S0-BMZ-974

ANCIENT EGYPT *as represented in the* MUSEUM OF FINE ARTS, BOSTON

ANCIENT EGYPT

as represented in the

MUSEUM OF FINE ARTS, BOSTON

By

WILLIAM STEVENSON SMITH, Ph.D.

Curator of Egyptian Art

COPYRIGHT © 1960 BY MUSEUM OF FINE ARTS, BOSTON 15, MASSACHUSETTS
FOURTH EDITION, FULLY REVISED.   LIBRARY OF CONGRESS CARD NO. 60–13944
DESIGNED BY CARL F. ZAHN   PRINTED IN U.S.A. BY T. O. METCALF CO., BOSTON

Preface to the First Edition

THE PRESENT VOLUME grew out of a scheme to produce an authoritative as well as a useful handbook on the Egyptian collections in the Museum of Fine Arts. Its preparation was entrusted to Dr. Smith, a scholar of distinction, a recognized authority, and, for some years, Dr. Reisner's first Assistant in the excavations at Giza. Inevitably, the book became more than a handbook, and is really a short history of the development of Egyptian culture and art, well illustrated with pieces in the Museum collections. Each historical period is discussed in general before the section which describes the pertinent material in the Museum. It will be useful to visitors to be sure, but equally useful to the students and teachers of Egyptian history and art.

Its appearance at this time is extremely apposite. Coming as it does so soon after the death of Dr. George Andrew Reisner, Curator of Egyptian Art at the Museum, and one of the world's greatest Egyptologists, its author likes to regard it as a tribute to this great scholar whose indefatigable labors and brilliant research have been the major factor in creating the collection which the Museum houses. Although Dr. Smith will publish shortly a much more exhaustive book on Egyptian sculpture, this one calls especial attention to the collection the Museum owes to Dr. Reisner, and which many regard as not the most extensive but perhaps the most distinguished outside of Cairo.

As Director of the Museum, I should like to express my gratitude to certain friends of the Museum who bore the cost of publication. Thanks are due first to Mrs. Charles Gaston Smith and her Group who donated roughly half the required sum. Similar help was received also from Mr. Dows Dunham, Mr. and Mrs. Edward Jackson Holmes, Dr. Francis T. Hunter, Mrs. Gardiner M. Lane, Miss Katharine W. Lane, and Mr. Arthur S. Musgrave. The Museum is deeply appreciative of this assistance at a time when so many demands are made upon every purse.

G. H. EDGELL, *Director*

Boston
September 23, 1942

Contents

Introduction and Bibliography

In PREPARING a fourth edition of *Ancient Egypt* the illustrations have been thoroughly revised. Worn-out cuts have been replaced by fresh views of familiar objects while occasionally the emphasis has been shifted to other important pieces. A number of objects placed on exhibition since 1952 seemed to demand illustration. Some of these have been selected from new acquisitions coming to the Museum through gift or purchase but others are the result of the study of material long in storage which has now been restored to a sound condition by our technical services. We have by no means completed the lengthy task of dealing adequately with the objects in fragile condition from the excavations carried on by the Museum for some forty years in Egypt. Over the years we have had reason to be grateful to Mr. William J. Young's laboratory for the expert collaboration upon which so much depends. It is a pity that there is no space for pictures of the condition before treatment of such things as the electrum sheaths (Fig. 109) or the toilet spoon (Fig. 88). The recently acquired painting of a lady on linen (Fig. 127) presents a vastly improved appearance after it had been cleaned and mounted by Mr. John A. Finlayson of the Department of Paintings. Miss Suzanne Chapman has also succeeded in flattening out and mounting another large painting on linen (No. 72.4723) which had remained rolled up since 1872 when it came to us with the gift of the Way Collection. The panel of Ramesses III with a court lady, an early example of the elaborate use of glass inlay (Fig. 98) is again the result of studying what at first appeared to be rather unpromising pieces that had been held in reserve.

Except for the addition of new material and revisions made necessary by recent discoveries which have affected the historical background, the text remains substantially the same as in earlier editions. The study of our expedition records in connection with the publication of the Museum's excavations continues to increase our information about this collection. The reader will find a number of alterations in the text which have resulted from this, for example in regard to the chronology of the Sudan in the Meroitic Period.

It is hoped that the map of Egypt and Nubia will prove a helpful addition. The following more compact and up-to-date bibliography has been substituted for that in the introduction to previous editions.

Opposite: The Judge Mehu.
End of Dyn. V

BIBLIOGRAPHY

ALDRED, C. *The Development of Egyptian Art*, London, 1952. Original Edition in 3 vols.: *Old Kingdom Art in Ancient Egypt*, London, 1949. *Middle Kingdom Art in Ancient Egypt*, London, 1950. *New Kingdom Art in Ancient Egypt in the Eighteenth Dynasty*, London, 1951.

BEVAN, E. *A History of Egypt Under the Ptolemaic Dynasty*, London, 1927.

BREASTED, J. H. *Ancient Records of Egypt*, Vols. I-V, Chicago, 1906-7.

CAPART, J. *L'Art égyptien*. 2 vols. Brussels, 1909, 1911. *Deuxième Partie: I, L'Architecture*, 1922. *II, La Statuaire*, 1948. *III, Les Arts Graphiques*, 1942. *IV, Les Arts mineurs*, 1947.

DAVIES, NINA M. and GARDINER, A. H. *Ancient Egyptian Paintings*, 3 vols. Chicago, 1936.

DRIOTON, É. and VANDIER, J. *Les Peuples de l'orient méditerranéen*, II. *L'Egypte* ('Clio'). 3rd ed. Paris, 1952.

DUNHAM, D. *The Royal Cemeteries of Kush*, Vols. I-IV. Cambridge and Boston, 1950-58.

——— *The Egyptian Department and its excavations*, Boston, 1958.

——— *Second Cataract Forts*, Vol. I, *Semna-Kumma* (in press).

EHRICH, R. W. (ed.). *Relative Chronologies in Old World Archaeology*, Chicago, 1954.

ERMAN, A. *The Literature of the Ancient Egyptians*, Translated by A. M. Blackman. London, 1927.

FRANKFORT, H. *Kingship and the Gods*, Chicago, 1948.

FRANKFORT, H., FRANKFORT, H. A., WILSON, J. A. and JACOBSEN, T. *Before Philosophy*, Harmondsworth, 1949. Original Edition: *The Intellectual Adventure of Ancient Man*. Chicago, 1946.

GARDINER, A. H. *Egyptian Grammar*, 3rd ed. London, 1957.

HAYES, W. C. *The Scepter of Egypt*, Vols. I-II, New York and Cambridge, 1953-1959.

LUCAS, E. *Ancient Egyptian Materials and Industries*. 3rd ed. London, 1948.

MILNE, J. G. *A History of Egypt under Roman Rule*. 3rd ed. London, 1924.

PORTER, B. and MOSS, R. *Topographical Bibliography of Ancient Hieroglyphic Texts, Reliefs and Paintings*. Vols. I-VII, Oxford, 1927-51.

PRITCHARD, J. B. (ed.). *Ancient Near Eastern Texts Relating to the Old Testament*. Princeton, 1950.

——— *The Ancient East in Pictures relating to the Old Testament*. Princeton, 1954.

REISNER, G. A. *A History of the Giza Necropolis*, Vols. I-II, Cambridge, 1946-55.

——— *Kerma, I-V, Harvard African Studies*, Vols. V-VI, Cambridge, 1923.

——— *Mycerinus*, Cambridge, 1931.

SCHÄFER, H. and ANDRAE, W. *Die Kunst des Alten Orients. (Propylaeon-kunstgeschichte*, Vol. II), Berlin, 1925. 3rd ed., 1942.

SMITH, W. S.   *The Art and Architecture of Ancient Egypt.* Baltimore, 1958.

———   *A History of Egyptian Sculpture and Painting in the Old Kingdom,* 2nd ed. Boston, 1949.

STEINDORFF, G. and SEELE, K.   *When Egypt Ruled The East.* 2nd ed. Chicago, 1957.

VANDIER, J.   *Manuel d'Archéologie égyptienne,* Vols. I-III, Paris, 1952-58.

———   *La Religion égyptienne.* 2nd ed. Paris, 1949.

WILSON, J. A.   *The Culture of Ancient Egypt.* Chicago, 1956. Original Edition: *The Burden of Egypt,* Chicago, 1951.

WINLOCK, H. E.   *Excavations at Deir el Baḥri.* New York, 1942.

The reader should also find it useful to consult the following articles in the *Bulletin of the Museum of Fine Arts,* listed by volume number, year and page, which deal with the Museum's excavations in Egypt and important individual objects:

GIZA: Old Kingdom. *Sculpture from Mycerinus Pyramid:* 9 (1911), p. 13; 33 (1935), p. 21; 48 (1950), p. 10. *Western Cemetery:* 5 (1907), p. 20 (Nofer, etc.); 11 (1913), p. 19 (Pen-meru), p. 53 (Senezem-ib Family); 13 (1915), p. 29 (Reserve Heads); 20 (1922), p. 25; 33 (1935), p. 69; 34 (1936), p. 96; 36 (1938), p. 26; 37 (1939), p. 29; 56 (1958), p. 56 (Mehu and Senezem-ib Family). *Eastern Cemetery:* 25, Special Supplement, May, 1927, p. 1; 26 (1928), p. 76; 27 (1929), p. 83; 30 (1932), p. 56; 51 (1953), p. 23 (all for Queen Hetep-heres I); 23 (1925), pp. 12, 28; 25 (1927), p. 64 (Chapel of Queen Meresankh III), p. 96 (Coffin of Queen Meresankh II); 32 (1934), p. 2 (Khufu-khaf, etc.); 34 (1936), p. 3 (Pair statuette of Meresankh III); 37 (1939), p. 42 (Bust of Prince Ankh-haf); 44 (1946), p. 23 (Gilded copper diadem).

SUDAN: *Kerma (Middle Kingdom to Hyksos):* 12 (1914), p. 9; 13 (1915), p. 71; 39 (1941), p. 7. *Cataract Forts (Middle-New Kingdom):* 23 (1925), p. 20; 27 (1929), p. 64; 28 (1930), p. 47; 29 (1931), p. 66. *Royal Shawabtis:* 49 (1951), p. 40. *Gebël Barkal Temples (Kushite):* 15 (1917), p. 25; 23 (1925), p. 17 (Atlanersa Altar). *Nuri (Kushite):* 16 (1918), p. 67; 43 (1945), p. 53 (Aspelta Sarcophagus). *El Kurru (Kushite):* 19 (1921) p. 21; 46 (1948), p. 98. *Meroë (Meroitic):* 21 (1923), p. 12; 23 (1925), p. 18; 46 (1948), p. 100.

PREDYNASTIC OBJECTS: 46 (1948), p. 64 (Hippopotamus).

OLD KINGDOM SCULPTURE: *Saqqarah Chapels:* 8 (1910), p. 19; 27 (1929), p. 36. *Khnum-baf (Ba-baf)* statuette: 37 (1939), p. 117. *Old Kingdom Portraits:* 41 (1943), p. 68. *Wooden statue of Methethy:* 46 (1948), p. 30.

MIDDLE KINGDOM OBJECTS: *Assiut Sculpture:* 3 (1905), p. 13. *El Bersheh objects:* 19 (1921), p. 43; 39 (1941), p. 10. *Royal Sculpture:* 26 (1928), p. 61. *Jewelry:* 39 (1941), p. 94.

NEW KINGDOM OBJECTS: *Medinet Habu Faience Tiles:* 6 (1908), p. 47; *Amarna Reliefs:* 34 (1936), p. 22; 35 (1937), p. 11. *Merenptah Statue:* 37 (1939), p. 6. *Horemheb Relief, Hatshepsut Obelisk:* 40 (1942), p. 42. *Dwarf Statuette:* 47 (1949), p. 9. *Amenhotep, Son of Hapu:* 47 (1949), p. 42. *Toilet Box:* 50 (1952), p. 74. *Head of Amenhotep II,* 52 (1954), pp. 11, 41. *Theban Tomb Relief:* 52 (1954), p. 84. *Painter's Sketch:* 56 (1958), p. 102.

LATE PERIOD: *Amulets:* 28 (1930), p. 117. *Sculpture:* 29 (1931), p. 104; 35 (1937), p. 70; 47 (1949), p. 21; 49 (1951), p. 69; 50 (1952), pp. 19, 49; 51 (1953), pp. 2, 80; 53 (1955), p. 80; *Bronzes,* 57 (1959), p. 48.

1. King Khasekhem(?). Dyn. II

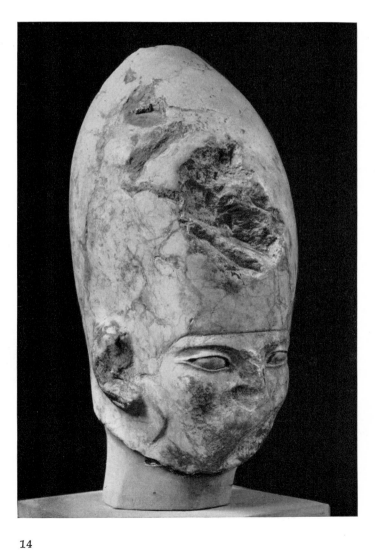

Chapter I

Egypt Before the Old Kingdom

THE EARLIEST APPEARANCE of man in the Nile Valley can be traced through the worked flints which hunters and herdsmen left on the upper terraces of the desert edge. The succeeding types of these weapons and tools correspond roughly to those of the Palaeolithic Period in Europe. In Neolithic times, in the period before 4000 B.C., early settlements began to appear on the lower gravel banks both in Upper and Lower Egypt.

The inhabitants of these villages were a mixed race as far back as can be discovered, combining elements from the west and east as well as some mixture from the south. With their advent into the Nile Valley commenced the transition from the wandering life of hunter and herdsman to that of settled agricultural communities. The very earliest settlements provide evidence for the cultivation of grain. The inhabitants of Merimde and the Fayum villages were already growing wheat, while fragments of woven linen show that the latter were also cultivating flax. The first settlers found the valley very different in appearance from what it is today. The annual inundation flooded a great portion of the land on each side of the river and after the water had receded swampy pools were left along the edge of the desert. Endless thickets of papyrus and reeds covered these marshy regions, and grew even more widely amongst the lagoons of the Delta. Land for cultivation had to be cleared little by little and the wild beasts that inhabited the swamps destroyed. Not only were there snakes and crocodiles to be feared, but the hippopotamus and elephant were still commonly met with. It is not surprising that formidable natural obstructions as well as diversity of origin should at first have isolated the tribes which settled in different places along the valley. We can see in these tribal units the origin of the various Nomes or Provinces which formed the underlying basis for the political structure of Egypt in historical times. However, the great river soon provided easy means of access between various localities along its banks and facilitated the striking uniformity of race, language, and culture which was to overshadow these individual peculiarities.

The great achievement of the prehistoric period was the control which was gained over the land. In order to do this it was necessary to curb in some way, and make use of, the inundation. Settling at first on stony outcrops above the alluvial plain, or on higher ground along the edge of the desert, the early Egyptians managed to clear the ground in their immediate neighborhood for cultivation, to fill in the swamps, and to build dikes against the incursions of the flood water. Gradually the use of canals for irrigation was learned. All this work required organized effort on a large scale, impossible for the individual alone, and led to the growth of a local political structure within each district.

Our knowledge of Predynastic Egypt at first depended upon the evidence supplied by a series of cemeteries in Upper Egypt. From the objects found in these graves the gradual development of the country could be traced through the Amratian and Gerzean Periods to the beginning of dynastic times. More recent excavations have produced traces of still earlier stages of primitive culture, not only in Upper Egypt at Tasa and Badari, but also in the north. The village of Merimde on the western edge of the Delta represents one of these early stages in man's development in the Nile Valley. To this are related the settlements in the Fayum and that of El Omari not far south of modern Cairo. They correspond roughly in time to those of Tasa and Badari in the south which preceded the Amratian culture. The very large settlement at Maadi is recognized as being later than the nearby site of El Omari and a few other sources of Predynastic objects are beginning to be known in the Eastern Delta. While much emphasis has been laid upon the differences between the cultures of Upper and Lower Egypt, assuming that greater progress was being made in the Delta, it must be remembered that at present a very small number of sites have been explored in the north. In general our knowledge of anything which preceded the Amratian culture of Upper Egypt rests upon a less secure basis than our familiarity with the latter, and must be amplified by further investigation.

The religious myths and writings concerned with kingly ritual which were gathered together in the Pyramid Texts seem frequently to hint at actual historical events. Although this material was not collected until late in Dynasty V when it is first found inscribed on the walls of the burial chamber of King Unas, portions of it are thought to be very much older. These fragments of early literary evidence reveal the growing political unity of Egypt, while emphasizing the distinction between Upper and Lower Egypt, which is apparent throughout historical times when at any weakening of the central authority the country tended to separate into two halves. At an early time the Nomes of the Delta seem to have formed themselves into coalitions. The western Nomes were traditionally united under the god Horus, while the eastern part of the Delta was joined under the god Anedjty, Lord of Djedu, who was later assimilated with the great god Osiris. Eventually the worship of Horus as the chief god prevailed throughout the Delta, and this has been taken to mean that the western Nomes conquered those of the east and formed a united northern kingdom. Nevertheless, Horus also maintained an early predominance in Upper Egypt where it has been supposed that he supplanted Seth who had his principal seat at Ombos. There has long been reason to doubt the theory that the Horus cult spread through conquest of the

South by the North and that this resulted in a Predynastic union of the whole country. We find that in late Gerzean times there were two separate kingdoms worshipping Horus, with Hierakonpolis as the capital of the South and Buto that of the Delta.

The unification of Egypt was traditionally assigned to Menes, the first king of Dynasty I. This great figure, although he was later recognized as the first truly historical personage, perhaps really unites the attributes of several kings, notably Narmer and Aha. Certainly it is the Southern Kingdom which now gains dominance over the whole country. Again, in Dynasty II, when there seems to have been a rebellion in the North, this was put down by the kings of Upper Egypt who revived the prestige of their old local god Seth, perhaps in order to strengthen their sectional unity. It would seem to have been the political organizing power of the strong, hardy people of the South which came forward throughout Egyptian history to solidify the country again after periods of disruption. Thus we see the Theban Kingdom reuniting Egypt in Dynasty XI after the chaos of the First Intermediate Period, and later driving out the Hyksos invaders in Dynasty XVII. It is with skepticism, therefore, that one views the suggestion of a Predynastic union of Egypt resulting from the military conquest of the south by the people of the Delta.

The culture of Predynastic Egypt shows us the transition from the use of stone implements to that of copper and the gradual development of the latter. Throughout Badarian and Amratian times the making of flint implements reached a stage of marvelous precision and skill, while copper, although known, appears only in small quantities which the craftsman was learning to utilize for practicable weapons and tools. With the Gerzean Period we begin to find the practical use of metal with all the possibilities of development in every craft which it implies, as well as the consequent decline of the flint industry. The influence of invention can be clearly seen in the rise and decline of other crafts. Thus the development of handmade pottery continues side by side with a somewhat limited working of stone vessels until toward the end of the Predynastic Period when the invention of the stone borer made the manufacture of splendid stone vessels much more rapid and cheap. There is then a gradual deterioration in the forms and decoration of pottery until the invention of the potter's wheel toward the end of Dynasty II caused the potter's craft to regain its ascendancy.

The first villages seem to have been formed mainly of reed shelters with an oval-shaped ground plan. These were open at one end and must have resembled the light constructions set up in the fields at the present day to protect the peasant from the hot noon sun and from the wind at night when he is camping out away from his village at harvesting time. In addition to these, the villager at Merimde sought additional protection for his sleeping place by hollowing out oval holes in the ground and banking them up with a rim of clods of patted mud. A pot sunk in the floor drained off any rain water that seeped in, while a hippopotamus bone served as a step down into the depression. Some kind of a matting roof must have covered this and in one case there was a cross pole to help support the layers of matting. Although the earliest huts of reed and wattle had a round or oval shape, by the Gerzean Period the ground plan became rectangular. In the settlement at Maadi small huts were built with a sheltering wall which projected out in front of the entrance to serve as a windbreak.

Although very little is left of these early buildings they give us a hint of what lay behind the quite elaborate system of architecture in mud brick and light materials which appears in Dynasty I. Of this little has survived except for the enormous brick tombs with their panelled outer walls which awaken our respect for the large scale of the work which the architect was prepared to undertake. Pictures of some of these early buildings appear in contemporary carvings, while the Dynasty III temples at the Saqqarah Step Pyramid show us this light construction quite literally translated into stone. The stone mason has imitated columns formed of mud-plastered bundles of reeds, palm-log ceilings, and mud-brick walls. Picket fences and projecting wooden elements were carved in relief in the small stone masonry. Even the wooden doors are shown, as though thrown back against the wall. Naive as is this adaptation into stone, the result is beautifully proportioned, light, and very pleasing. It represents a sophisticated architectural development in the handling of brick, wood, and light materials. The proficiency of the stonecutter which enabled Zoser's architect to execute this daring conception entirely in stone was apparently a Memphite development. Even as early as Dynasty I the workmen had learned how to cut chambers in the rock for the large tombs at Saqqarah, while across the river at Helwan large slabs of masonry were used to line the burial chambers. Perhaps more remarkable is the flooring of granite blocks in the central chamber of the tomb of Wedymu at Abydos. The Palermo Stone records a temple built of stone by King Khasekhemuwy at the end of Dynasty II, while that king's tomb has the burial chamber built of small limestone blocks, although the rest of the construction is of brick. A large door-jamb of granite executed for this king at Hierakonpolis is even decorated with reliefs. Such work in hard stone is an achievement more to be expected in Dynasty IV or V than in the archaic period. It makes one realize how much we have still to learn about the architecture of Dynasties I and II.

OBJECTS OF THE PREDYNASTIC PERIOD

THE LIFE of the early settlers of Lower Egypt is reflected in the Museum of Fine Arts collection by objects of daily use found in the prehistoric settlement of Merimde on the western edge of the Delta. The stone weapons and tools look clumsy and primitive compared to the beautifully chipped flint implements of the Amratian Period. Rough pottery vessels made in a few simple shapes were used for cooking and for carrying and storing water. A broken piece shows that some of the bowls had supporting feet, a practical contrivance which seems to have been used only by the people of the Delta. The two flat stones for grinding grain,

2. Pottery of the Amratian Period

3. Predynastic Slate Palettes

as well as a handful of wheat blackened by age, tell us that even these earliest villagers were already an agricultural people.

In early Predynastic times the potter had learned how to make well-shaped vessels with a red polished surface and burned to a shiny black inside and around the top. Ordinarily this black-topped ware was not decorated, but the figure of a mountain sheep has been scratched on the side of a tall beaker from Abadiyeh in Fig. 2. Geometric patterns are found on black polished pottery like the bowl in Fig. 2. The zigzag lines, crosshatchings, and dots are incised into the surface and filled with white paint. The designs imitate basket-work patterns. A wider range of patterns including plants, animals and, more rarely, human figures, was painted in creamy white on the red polished surface of another class of vessels. Occasionally plastic ornament was added as in the clumsy animals which are modelled as though standing on the rim of the tall jar (Fig. 2). Although the black-topped vases continued to be made, these decorated wares disappear at the end of the Amratian Period. Their place is taken by a finer buff-colored pottery with somewhat similar designs in red paint. Such is the tall jar in Fig. 7 with its many-oared boats. On other vases flamingoes, desert animals, and human figures are grouped around the boats while the empty spaces are filled with zigzag lines and plant forms. The angular, geometric forms are indicated by strokes and blobs of paint and are in style like the earliest of the Egyptian wall paintings found in a tomb of the late Gerzean Period at Hierakonpolis and now in the Cairo Museum. The emblems on the standards in the boats resemble those which later belonged to the different Nomes or provinces of Egypt. Although writing did not yet exist, the use of these tribal emblems probably represents one of the first steps toward its invention.

The craftsman was not only learning how to fashion vessels from stone, but he was able to carve from hard slate quite passable imitations of various animals for the paint palettes which were much in demand. On the vigorously worked little lions, elephants, turtles, hippopotami, or fish the Egyptians ground the green malachite for their eye-paint (Fig. 3). It was perhaps through this use of malachite that they became familiar with the copper that it contained. The attraction of gold as an ornament probably led to the working of metals which resulted in the practical use of this copper for weapons and tools.

Sculpture in the round began with small, crude human figures of mud, clay, and ivory (Fig. 4). The faces are pinched out of the clay until they have a form like the beak of a bird. Arms and legs are long rolls attached to the slender bodies of men, while the hips of the women's figures are enormously exaggerated. A greater variety of attitudes and better workmanship are found in the ivory figurines which sometimes have the eye indicated by the insertion of a bead (Fig. 4). It is the carving of animals, however, such as the ivory hippopotamus from Mesaeed in Fig. 4, or the pottery figure (Fig. 6) which points the way toward the rapid advance which was to be made in the Hierakonpolis ivories and in the small carvings of Dynasty I.

4. Predynastic Figures

5. Archaic ivory carvings and faience from Abydos and Hierakonpolis

THE ARCHAIC PERIOD

THE KINGS of the first three dynasties still remain to us rather nebulous figures, nor can we learn much concerning the events of individual reigns. The badly smashed equipment from the Abydos tombs of Dynasties I and II gives evidence of a brilliant and luxurious court. The little British Museum plaque with the picture of Wedymu striking down an ' Easterner ' dramatically represents a dominance over the nomadic tribes which was to lead to the control of the Sinai Peninsula under the kings of Dynasty III. Narmer at the beginning of Dynasty I stands out as a personality in the scenes on the ceremonial palette in the Cairo Museum which evidently records a military triumph over the people of the Delta. Khasekhem we know, in Dynasty II, from his two splendid portrait statues in the Cairo Museum and at Oxford which again suggest, by the pictures on their bases, conflict with the North. A royal head recently added to our collection strongly resembles those of Khasekhem and may be another portrait of him (Fig. 1). At the end of Dynasty II the monuments of Khasekhemuwy seem to represent a definite stride forward in culture which was to be realized more fully in Dynasty III by the marvelous architecture of the Step Pyramid and its surrounding complex of temples. The forceful face of the statue of Zoser in Cairo suggests the power of the man who was responsible for this achievement. The other kings of Dynasty III are as shadowy as those of the first two dynasties, although the newly discovered Step Pyramid at Saqqarah of Zoser's successor, Sekhem-khet, and the immense excavation of the unfinished tomb of another king at Zawiyet el Aryan are sufficient to prove that Zoser was not alone as a great builder. The monuments of Sekhem-khet and Sa-nekht in Sinai suggest that they as well as Zoser carried the fear of Egyptian arms amongst the wild eastern tribes. The last king, Huni, is no more than a name to us, but with the reign of Sneferu we begin to have a clearer picture of Egyptian civilization, which had now reached the first of its great periods of achievement.

OBJECTS OF THE ARCHAIC PERIOD

THE PROGRESS of the sculptor of small objects in Early Dynastic times is brilliantly illustrated by the objects from the royal tombs at Abydos. If one compares the delicate hand from a statuette, the bull's legs from a box, or the headless figure of the lioness in Fig. 5 with the Predynastic figurines in Fig. 4, the greatly improved modelling and the skill in handling the material are immediately apparent. The wider variety of forms is suggested by the bearded man, the woman with her hands on her breast, and the well carved but badly preserved squatting figure in Fig. 5. Similarly, the green-glazed faience objects in Fig. 5, while lacking the delicate detail of the ivory carvings, show the increasing ability of the sculptors who made the small human and animal figures which were placed as votive offerings in the temples at Abydos and Hierakonpolis.

6. Amratian pottery hippopotamus

7. Gerzean painted jar

8. Stone vase of King Khasekhemuwy
   with gold cover, Abydos

The furniture placed in the royal tombs of Dynasties I and II was of the richest materials and most sophisticated workmanship. The making of stone vessels had reached a point where highly fantastic shapes were attempted. Fragmentary examples of these are the pieces of a marble dish imitating woven basketwork (No. 01.7286) or another fragment with delicately carved designs like embossed metal (No. 01.7299). The small faience cup in Fig. 5 is a cheaper imitation of a composite version known elsewhere with slate sepals and alabaster petals. For ordinary use were the two plain bowls excavated by the Museum's Expedition in the cemetery beside the peculiar layer pyramid of Zawiyet el Aryan. They are unusual, however, in having scratched inside them the name of the little-known King Kha-ba of Dynasty III. The stone vase of Khasekhemuwy, the last king of Dynasty II, has a gold cover imitating a cloth laid over the top of the jar and tied with a string (Fig. 8). It was one of several similar vases overlooked in the pillage and suggests how great the wealth of these tombs must have been before they were robbed. So also does the sceptre of the same king, made of lengths of sard fitted on a copper tube and separated by bands of gold (No. 01.7285). This is only one section of the sceptre, another piece of which is in the Cairo Museum. The small faience element with a hawk standing on a frame representing the palace-façade came from the tomb of a Dynasty I queen near Giza. It is part of a bracelet like that of the wife of King Zer in the Cairo Museum.

The cutting of reliefs in hard stone had gained even greater dexterity than sculpture in the round at the beginning of Dynasty I. The Cairo Museum possesses the finest of these early reliefs in the slate palette of King Narmer. The royal stelae set up at the king's tombs at Abydos, although simpler in design, show equally fine workmanship. The same cannot be said of the small grave stela of a court lady buried in one of the little tombs surrounding that of King Zer (No. 01.7294). The craftsmen available to the private person had not been able to keep pace with the rapid strides being made in the royal workshops. There is something pathetically appealing about the laborious chiselling and uneven surfaces of this simple figure. Her name is haltingly written above her head in the new hieroglyphic language which the king's sculptors were already employing with superb decorative effect. Unpromising as this small stela seems, it has an honorable position as one of the first of a long line of private monuments among which were to be found the splendid chapel reliefs of the Old Kingdom.

Chapter II

The Old Kingdom

THE HISTORICAL BACKGROUND OF DYNASTIES IV TO VI

THE GREAT KINGS of Dynasty IV are known to us chiefly through their building activities. Although the architecture, sculpture, and painting of the period are familiar to us, scarcely any record of historical events has survived from the reigns of Sneferu and his successors. We know the names and faces of the important people of the time, even a little about their private lives, but although we can guess from their titles something about the parts that they played in public life, we have only tantalizing glimpses of the events in which they found themselves involved.

We know that Sneferu sent an expedition to Sinai where a rock carving shows him striking down one of the local Bedouin chiefs. In this he was following in the footsteps of his predecessors of Dynasty III who left records there. Sneferu's son Cheops also had a bas-relief carved at the Wady Maghara, but there are no further memorials of expeditions until that of Sahura early in Dynasty V. The Sinai reliefs probably represent military expeditions sent out to put down the lawless tribes of the eastern desert and to protect the important mining operations for turquoise. Cheops also made use of the diorite quarries in a waterless place far out in the Nubian desert about fifty miles west of Abu Simbel. From there came the beautiful stone which Chephren used for his statues. Radedef and Sahura, as well as Cheops, left stelae recording expeditions to these quarries.

A military raid against the Nubians is recorded in Sneferu's Annals on the Palermo Stone. This may have been sufficient to ensure the peaceful working of the diorite quarries in the following reigns, or there may have had to be a continued show of military force in the south. We do not know. Mention is also made in the Annals of the building of 100-ell ships of mer-wood and cedar, which suggests regular traffic with the Syrian coast to bring back cedar of Lebanon. Probably the port of call was Byblos, as in later times, for a fragment of a stone vessel bearing the name of Khasekhemuwy was found there, showing that the trade was already in existence at the end of Dynasty II. A heavy copper axe-head with the name of a boat crew, probably of Cheops, was found at the mouth of the river Adonis not far from Byblos, while excavations at the port have produced other objects inscribed with the names of Chephren and Mycerinus.

Sneferu reigned for 24 years according to the Turin Papyrus, while a document of the Middle Kingdom, the Admonitions to an otherwise unknown Vizier of Dynasty III, Kagemni, states that Sneferu succeeded to the throne at the death of Huni. It is very probable that the new king was the son of a secondary queen and that he legitimized his position by marrying Hetep-heres I, who, if she were the eldest daughter of Huni, as is probable, would have carried the blood royal over to the new dynasty. This lady outlived Sneferu and was buried by her son Cheops, probably beside her husband's pyramid at Dahshur. The tomb did not remain long undisturbed and the queen's body was destroyed by the robbers who broke into the chamber. A clever prime minister seems to have been able to convince Cheops that little damage had been done. He ordered the lid of the alabaster coffin replaced to hide the absence of the queen's body, and the greater part of the unharmed burial equipment was moved to a secret burial shaft in front of the Great Pyramid in the new cemetery at Giza. Cheops apparently never discovered the ruse practised upon him by his minister, for he made an offering to his mother's spirit before the shaft was finally closed. The secret was not disclosed until the intact chamber was opened by the Harvard-Boston Expedition in 1925, revealing its amazing treasure of gold-covered furniture and personal equipment that had been presented to the queen by her husband and son.

The long and prosperous reign of Cheops seems to have ended in a palace intrigue of which we have the barest hint in the inscriptions of the beautiful painted chapel of his granddaughter, Queen Meresankh III. Her mother, Hetep-heres II, was married to the Crown Prince Ka-wab who was very probably murdered by Radedef, a son of one of the lesser wives of Cheops. Radedef married Hetep-heres, evidently in an effort to compensate her for the loss of her husband and throne. The marriage can hardly have been a successful one, for another wife had already borne Radedef a son, thus relegating the new queen to a minor position. Radedef disappears from the scene after a short reign of eight years, leaving unfinished the pyramid which he had started at Abu Roash. Hetep-heres herself joined the party which brought a brother of her first husband to the throne, and married the daughter whom she had borne to Ka-wab to the new king Chephren. Hints of this fraternal strife between the children of the various queens of Cheops are evident in the Giza cemetery in the unfinished tombs and in the malicious erasure of the inscriptions of certain members of the family. This trouble was probably not completely resolved upon the accession of Chephren, and it is very likely that the descendants of Radedef made several attempts to regain the throne. They may in fact have been the final cause of the downfall of the dynasty. According to one of the reconstructions of the Turin Papyrus, which is fragmentary at this point, one of them may have been able to seize the throne for a brief time at the close of the reign of Chephren, before his son Mycerinus had succeeded in establishing himself in control of the country. Another may possibly have followed the last real king of the dynasty, Shepseskaf.

The legend of later times in the Westcar Papyrus, which relates that the first three kings of Dynasty V were the offspring of the god Ra and a lady named Radedet, wife of a priest at Heliopolis, seems to suggest that the new dynasty came into being as the result of the growing strength of the priesthood of Heliopolis. Although the title of ' Son of Ra ' had already been adopted by Chephren in the preceding dynasty, the constant use of this title, the records of temple building and endowment inscribed on the Palermo Stone, and above all the introduction of the Sun Temple into the funerary cult, seem to support this idea. Just what position the Queen Mother, Khent-kawes, assumed in the transition from one dynasty to another is by no means clear. Her titles indicate great importance, while the building of a large tomb of unusual form at Giza shows close association with the older royal family. It is possible that Weserkaf married her in order to strengthen his position on the throne, just as Sneferu had married Hetep-heres I. The Westcar Papyrus makes Weserkaf the brother of Sahura, and Neferirkara, but the last two may be sons of Weserkaf and Khent-kawes. Weserkaf built his pyramid beside Zoser's Step Pyramid at Saqqarah. The plan of the temple is more like those of Dynasty IV than the elaborate structures which his successors erected at Abusir. It was decorated with magnificent reliefs, of which unfortunately only fragments remain. His building activities extended as far as Tod in the Theban Nome, where a column has been found inscribed with his name.

Sahura is chiefly known for the splendid reliefs which decorated his funerary temple at Abusir. These show the booty which was brought back from raids against the Libyans of the western desert and the Asiatics in the east. Large ships filled with bearded foreigners indicate that one of these expeditions was carried out by sea, as do similar representations in the temple of Unas, at the end of the dynasty, and the raid on southern Palestine mentioned in the biography of Weni in the reign of Pepy I of Dynasty VI. The reliefs of Unas actually show a battle between Egyptians and men who look like Bedouins of the eastern desert, while two private tombs of Dynasty VI picture Egyptians besieging small walled towns, one apparently defended by Libyans and the other by Asiatics. The Palermo Stone mentions offerings from Mafket Land (Sinai) and Punt (the Somali Coast) brought for the temple of Hathor in the reign of Sahura. Expeditions to Punt for the incense so necessary in temple ritual are mentioned frequently in Dynasty VI inscriptions, but one of these refers back to an earlier expedition in Dynasty V. The boy king Pepy II writing to Harkhuf concerning the care of the dancing dwarf which he is bringing back from Wawat mentions that the like has not occurred since the Vizier Ba-wer-djed, on an expedition to the land of Punt, procured for Isesy a similar dwarf from the ' Land of Spirits.' Most of the kings of Dynasty V have recorded their expeditions to Sinai in rock carvings on the cliffs of the Wady Maghara.

Thus we find the rulers of the later Old Kingdom able to penetrate farther into the surrounding countries, although probably only for the purpose of furthering trade and protecting their borders. Nubia must have been well under the control

27

of the kings of Dynasty IV, however, to permit the working of the diorite quarries which were reached from some point in the Nile Valley near Abu Simbel. Just what the relations with Byblos were is not certain. An Egyptian temple seems to have been established there as early as Dynasty IV, and the port was apparently open to Egyptian shipping throughout the Old Kingdom for the export of the much-desired cedar wood. Whether Egypt exerted some political control over this town or simply kept up friendly trade connections is quite unknown.

Toward the end of Dynasty IV brief biographical inscriptions began to appear in the tombs. While these are more specific than the early account which Methen left of his administrative career in the Delta, they still give us little in the way of historical record. Most of them recount the special favor of the king, such as his inspection of the writer's tomb, the presentation of tomb equipment, or the advancement in office of the recipient. Many of the inscriptions refer to building works executed for the king, particularly those of the Senezem-ib family which held the office of royal architect and overseer of the king's works from the reign of Isesy to that of Pepy II. In Dynasty VI the biography of Weni and those of the caravan leaders of Aswan give a more complete picture of the conduct of trade with the south and operations against the Bedouin tribes in the east during the reigns of Pepy I, Mernera, and Pepy II. We gain an impression of the growing power of the Nomarchs of Upper Egypt in Dynasty VI from the inscriptions in their tombs, which are now made in their own districts and not at the capital. A rapidly increasing process of decentralization was taking place. The king was losing direct control, while more and more power passed into the hands of the powerful provincial leaders, who set up smaller local units of government imitating the Memphite court and more and more loosely controlled by it. Thus the energetic Nomarchs of Elephantine were largely responsible for the exploration and colonization of Nubia which was developed to a great extent in Dynasty VI.

The enormous building projects of the Old Kingdom and the gradual dissipation of the property of the crown through the gifts of funerary endowments to favorites of the king had decreased the royal wealth to an alarming degree. The gradual equalization of wealth had increased to such a point by the end of the dynasty that the king's power was dangerously weakened. The very long reign of Pepy II, one of the longest in history, came to an end in political confusion. The complete impoverishment of the royal house is plain from the absence of monuments after those of Pepy II. As disintegration rapidly set in, this impoverishment spread throughout all classes of society.

An ephemeral Dynasty VII, of which there is no evidence except in Manetho's King List, gave way to Dynasty VIII, of which we have little record except for the names of certain kings whose order is disputed. That Memphite traditions were carried on is shown by the continuation of some tombs at Saqqarah and the small pyramid of Aba with texts in its burial chamber like those of Dynasty VI. Soon a new royal house managed to set itself up at Heracleopolis and made some attempt to carry on Memphite culture. These kings were evidently able to control the Delta, which had been a prey to marauding desert tribes, as we learn from the instructions of a king, whose name has been lost, to his son King Meri-kara. Upper Egypt had split up into its old tribal units, each Nome under the control of its local ruler. Conditions in every district seem to have been bad, judging from the poverty of the tombs which these Nomarchs prepared for themselves in the neighborhood of their local capitals. Certain decrees set up at Coptos indicate the dependence of the Memphite kings of Dynasty VIII upon the loyalty of the rulers of this Nome which was soon to join forces with the rising power of the Theban Nome. The subsequent history of Egypt is concerned with the growth of this Theban power which in Dynasty XI was destined to gain control first of Upper Egypt, and not very long afterwards of the whole country.

RELIGIOUS BELIEFS AND THEIR EFFECT UPON EGYPTIAN ART

THE BELIEFS of the Egyptian people concerning a life after death were responsible for the principal characteristics of Egyptian art. Representation in sculpture and painting was employed as a magical means by which life could be re-created for the dead man. The early Egyptians imagined that life would continue after death much as it had in this world, and at first it seemed to them only necessary to provide a secure burial for the protection of the body and to place in the grave a supply of food and drink with perhaps a few items of personal equipment. The recitation of prayers addressed especially to the god of the dead, Anubis, was thought to provide magically for the transformation of these objects into supplies for the spirit and to ensure their continuance. Gradually an elaborate cult of the dead was built up around these simple beginnings. The effort to protect the dead resulted in such vast architectural projects as the pyramid of the Old Kingdom surrounded by its accompanying field of lesser tombs, or the laboriously tunnelled tombs in the Valley of the Kings and the mortuary temples of the New Kingdom. Paintings and reliefs were employed upon the chapel walls first to represent supplies of food with the appropriate prayers to make them available to the dead, and later to show the preparation of this food, the agricultural processes, the capture of game, and the raising of cattle and domestic fowl. Here also were represented pleasant scenes from life, feasting, dancing, and singing, the inspection of the wealth of a great estate, that these might be transformed into reality in the Afterworld. Statues were made and placed in the tomb in order to provide permanent residing places for the soul of the dead man, substitutes in case the body itself should be destroyed.

In the early Old Kingdom this cult of the dead was associated only with the god Anubis, the Lord of the Dead, and with the 'Great God' of the universe, a heavenly or world deity who had been merged with the state god Horus after the uniting of Egypt at the beginning of Dynasty I. Since the king was the personification of the 'Living Horus,' the mention of the 'Great God' in the tomb-prayers may refer both to the king and to the universal god. The dead man was not associated with any other gods in the tomb pictures, nor in the texts concerned with providing for his sustenance after death. The feasts of Thoth, Sokar, and Min mentioned in these texts were not primarily concerned with the cult of the dead but were festivals of the living at which offerings were also presented to the dead. It is not until the middle of Dynasty V that the Osiris legends, which expressed so well the idea of resurrection and after life, came to be associated with the funerary beliefs of the individual. Then this god began to take his place beside Anubis in the prayers and soon was thought of as the principal deity of the dead.

In his daily life the Egyptian believed that his actions were vitally affected by the gods. These were friendly or hostile spirits which had to be propitiated, but there were also the great impersonal powers of nature which did not concern themselves with man. The local village gods in the original tribal divisions of the country had been largely personifications of the various aspects of nature whose power became more general as their districts grew politically. Thus Horus, by the military prowess of the clan that worshipped him, became a national god, displacing his powerful rival Seth, while Wazet and Nekhbet, the goddesses of Buto and Nekheb, the old capitals of the Kingdoms of the North and the South, came to be tutelary deities of the royal house of the United Kingdom. The emblems of the different Nomes indicate how gods, originally all-powerful in their own locality, have been replaced by other gods who absorbed certain of their attributes, or have themselves been transferred to other districts. We can see how Min, the god of fertility, was brought early from Akhmim to Coptos where he replaced the local god, or how the ibis-headeed Thoth, god of wisdom and of writing, came from the Delta to Hermopolis which became the chief seat of his worship. The ram-headed Khnum, patron god of the potters, is associated both with Antinoë and the cataract region, and perhaps also under the name of Her-shef with Heracleopolis. In the Old Kingdom, Hathor, the goddess of love, had two principal seats of worship, at Denderah and at Cusae, but Neith, the protectress of warriors and hunters, always made her home at Sais. At Heliopolis, Ra, the sun god, absorbed an older deity, Atum. Ptah, under whose special care were the artists and craftsmen, was always associated with Memphis.

These were the most important gods of the Old Kingdom and it is interesting to see how, as their power extended beyond their original sphere of influence, they assumed various aspects of the great cosmic spirits of nature. Thus while Nut borrowed the cow form from Hathor, the latter assumed from her (Nut) the properties of a sky goddess. Thoth absorbed the powers of the Moon God Yoh, while Horus, Ra, Osiris, and Ptah tended to be merged with the all-pervading spirit of the universe, the 'Great God.' Learned priests early attempted to relate their city gods in an orderly scheme, arranging them according to rank. They sought, whenever possible, to place at the head of the system a family group consisting of the chief god, his consort goddess, and their son. The theologians of Heliopolis also worked out a system for the spirits of the powers of nature through which they explained the creation of the world. In this, the self-created Ra, author of the Universe, produced a divine pair Shu, the god of the air and his wife Tefnut, the spirit of moisture. From these were born Geb, the god of the earth, and Nut, the goddess of the sky, who in turn produced Osiris and his wife Isis, as well as Seth and his wife Nephthys. A rival theory of the creation which was maintained at Hermopolis, the home of Thoth the god of wisdom, saw in Nun, the god of the primaeval waters, the creator of a similar system of cosmic gods to which belonged Amon. These were the eight gods of Hermopolis as opposed to the nine of Heliopolis. The priests of Memphis later contributed a third and far more spiritual creed by which Atum originated as thought in the heart of Ptah and found his way through Ptah's tongue into all human beings and animals. Nevertheless, the more primitive doctrine of Heliopolis managed to hold its own throughout Egyptian history.

The problem which confronted the king after death was different from that of the ordinary man. It was complicated by the fact that as a personification of Horus, and certainly from the time of Chephren as the ' Son of Ra,' he must take his place among the gods after death. Not only that, but he was to be their chief for he was thought to become one with the sun god Ra. From the middle of Dynasty V on it was thought that he also became Osiris. In order to assist the king in achieving this end the priests composed a long series of magical texts and spells which were inscribed upon the walls of the burial chamber of his pyramid. Although these were compiled only toward the end of Dynasty V, they represent the long-accumulated lore of the Heliopolitan priesthood. With the texts concerning the sun god Ra are inextricably mixed the newer myths of the god Osiris, his destruction by his brother Seth and his resurrection brought about through the faithful services of his wife Isis and their son Horus.

In the troubled period after the Old Kingdom, the Pyramid Texts, which had been composed solely for the service of the king, were usurped by the great provincial chieftains who were like petty kings in their own districts. In this way the texts came to be engraved upon the coffin of any wealthy person of the Middle Kingdom who could afford proper burial equipment. Great confusion of ideas resulted from this, for the texts were altered only slightly as new material was added to them. Not only did they contain the mixture of Sun cult and Osiris belief, but their royal terminology was hardly suitable for a private person. It is doubtful whether the nobleman of the Middle Kingdom thought that he would become one of the gods after death, as the king of the Old Kingdom may be supposed to have believed. These texts were simply to ensure the man a safe place in the Afterworld. It is significant of the growing skepticism and doubt, that men should grasp at such possible means of protection as the coffin texts. The dependence upon magical spells and amuletic charms was to grow more pronounced in the New Kingdom. Then we find the coffin texts transformed and amplified into the Book of the Dead with its terrible Underworld peopled by fantastic demons against which a very complicated magic had to be employed.

From the beginning, then, representational art was employed largely in the service of the cult of the dead and for religious purposes. It was necessary to build enduring temples for the gods as well as tombs for the dead, while statues of the deities, large and small, served as residing places for their spirits just as a man's statue provided a place for his *ka* or spirit. The statues of the gods were clothed and fed and plied with incense just as were the statues of the dead. Therefore, in representing both gods and men, we find naturalism and enduring qualities as the chief aims of the artist. The Egyptian was also influenced by an attitude toward the world about him which was common to all peoples before the development of Greek culture. The artist sought to show things as he knew them to be, not in their transitory aspects. Because of this and because of the purpose for which his work was intended, we need not expect the impulse toward naturalism to lead the Egyptian further than a certain point. For example he did not attempt to imitate movement in statues or to represent complicated groupings of figures. The ideal for which he was striving was achieved by the sculptors of Dynasty IV. Later craftsmen might, and did, improve upon the details of such sculpture, but the compact, static mass of the figures, the elimination of unnecessary accessories, and above all the lifelike quality of the portraiture, enhanced by painted surfaces and inlaid eyes, provided admirably what was demanded of the sculptor by his patron.

The draughtsman, on the other hand, produced a kind of diagrammatic rendering of a mental picture which served his purpose well as a re-creation of this world for the soul after death. Thus we can expect no development in Egyptian reliefs and painting toward the representation of a complete visual effect such as we have come to look for in Western painting, but rather the technical perfection of a craft within certain boundaries established as an early developed means of expressing ideas. These diagrams must be interpreted by our knowledge of what the artist is trying to represent, but the Egyptian's inherent sense of balance and proportion and his fine feeling for line make his work pleasing to the eye even before we understand his meaning. Finally, it should be observed that within the general boundaries of convention there was considerable room for variety resulting from the Egyptian's natural powers of observation. We must not think of Egyptian art as endlessly repeating and imitating the same forms.

The individual artist in ancient Egypt was of little importance. His standing resulted from his proficiency as a craftsman. However, although there was small opportunity for the artist to stamp his own personal qualities upon his work, he did not remain entirely anonymous. It is really surprising to consider how many names of artists we do know, but when we attempt to identify their contributions to the work with which their names are associated, it becomes evident that we can recognize only certain schools of craftsmen in which they are merged. The differences between these schools is by no means easy to distinguish, but once the general style of the time has been established, it is possible to observe individual variations that occur within each period and in a few rare instances to note the influence which has been exerted by some artist of special ability.

THE SCULPTURE AND MINOR ARTS OF THE OLD KINGDOM

THE SCULPTURE of Dynasty IV forms a splendid culmination to that long period of development which began with the small carvings of the Predynastic Period. Although the rare examples of statues and reliefs which illustrate the transitional steps in this development can only be seen to advantage in Egypt itself or in a few European collections, the Museum of Fine Arts is unusually fortunate in being able to exhibit a large number of masterpieces of the great period of Memphite art from its excavations at Giza. These are fully supplemented by sculpture of Dynasties V and VI and by a wealth of material illustrating the minor arts of the Old Kingdom.

Not long after construction had started on his great pyramid at Giza, Cheops ordered work begun on two large cemeteries for his family and courtiers. The size of this undertaking is evident from the fact that the cemetery west of the pyramid (Fig. 9) contained 64 large tombs, the stone corework of which was

9. The excavated cemetery west of Cheops' pyramid at Giza

10. Reserve Head of Prince buried in
Giza Tomb 4440

11. Head of Prince's wife, G 4440

probably all completed during the king's lifetime. The Eastern Field contained a smaller number of tombs, but the eight mastabas that formed the nucleus of this cemetery were truly enormous. These were constructed toward the close of the king's reign and were intended for his favorite children. Other large tombs were added to these in subsequent reigns. The earliest stone mastabas in the Western Cemetery were equipped with comparative simplicity. The walls of the brick chapel which was built against the east face of the mastaba were covered with whitewash. Apparently the only decoration was an inscribed tablet set in the stepped face of the mastaba core and framed by a brick niche in the west wall of the chapel. These so-called slab-stelae were gifts presented as a mark of ownership of the tomb by the king himself. They are executed in fine low relief and beautifully painted. That of the Princess Merytyetes (No. 12.1510), although it has lost its color, illustrates very well the delicate modelling of the low relief. The princess is shown seated at a table of bread with a list of food, drink, and personal equipment arranged in separate compartments. With a few modifications this was to become the traditional scene that was placed on the tablet of the offering niche when this was in the form of a stone false-door.

Although, with one exception, the statues which must have been placed in these early Cheops chapels have not been preserved, a series of wonderful portrait heads has escaped destruction. These did not form part of a statue, but were complete in themselves and were placed in the burial chamber with the mummy, probably to serve as a substitute for the head in case the mummy should be destroyed. Since the statues of Cheops himself have disappeared except for a few fragments and a tiny ivory statuette in Cairo, these heads, undoubtedly executed by a master sculptor of the king, are unusually precious. With the Hildesheim seated statue of Prince Hemiunu, the one complete early statue recovered at

12. Portrait of Princess, G 4540   13. Prince from Giza 4140

Giza, and the famous pair of Rahotep and Nofret from Medum in Cairo, they give us an unusually vivid impression of the aristocratic members of the court. The makers of these white limestone heads have seized expertly the salient features of the person portrayed. The planes of the face are simplified but a strong feeling of individuality is maintained in the calm, dignified features. Unlike most Egyptian sculpture, these heads do not appear to have been painted.

The aquiline type of face so characteristic of some of the members of the Cheops family appears in the head of the prince from G 4440 (Fig. 10). A petulant expression about the mouth and an irregularity of feature which suggests weakness differentiate this face from the other male heads, such as that of the Treasurer Nofer (Fig. 14). Nofer, who in spite of the facial resemblance did not belong to the royal family, represents quite a different type from the handsome man shown in Fig. 13. The more regular features of the latter give him a conventional appearance that is probably misleading. Although we do not know his name, he was married to the Princess Merytyetes whose slab-stela was described above. The wife of the other unknown Prince (G 4440) is of negroid type with thick lips, wide nostrils, and full cheeks (Fig. 11). The sculptor has adopted a broad, impressionistic treatment, particularly in the area around the eyes. Altogether different is the piquant head of a princess (Fig. 12) with her delicate features and sharp upturned nose.

In spite of their individuality, however, these heads belong to a school of sculpture which, prompted by restrained idealism, shows a tendency to summarize and to work in broad-surfaced planes. This can be seen more clearly after examining the work of another school that appeared in the following reign. These younger sculptors employed a more plastic treatment of the surfaces which finds its most striking expression in the bust of Ankh-haf (Fig. 17).

14. Reserve head of Nofer

15. Door-jamb of Nofer's chapel

16. Bowmen of King's bodyguard, Old Kingdom royal temple relief

That the best artists of the Old Kingdom were really trying to capture a recognizable likeness of their patrons is emphasized by the resemblance between the reserve head of Nofer (Fig. 14) and a portrait in relief from his chapel. The prominent nose and peculiar shape of the lips and chin have been imitated well in the face of the figure on the entrance jamb (Fig. 15). The likeness fades into conventionality in the head from another wall. A further striking resemblance is that between the head of Hemiunu (Fig. 20) on a fragment of relief from his chapel and that of the seated statue of the prince in Hildesheim.

The reliefs of Hemiunu and Nofer are from the stone chapels which towards the end of the reign of Cheops began to replace the mud-brick offering rooms of the earliest mastabas. The very finest low relief was employed in the chapel of Hemiunu. It is similar in quality to that of the slab-stelae and to the rarely preserved temple reliefs of the reign of Cheops, of which we have some fragments from the chapel of one of the queens' pyramids. Until recently no reliefs were known from the pyramid temples of Dynasty IV. Their use was questioned because it was thought that the walls were cased with granite as was the interior of the Valley Temple of the Second Pyramid. Fragments of fine relief carved in white limestone and bearing the name of the king and that of his pyramid have now been found in the Cheops temple. Others were discovered, reused, in a Middle Kingdom pyramid at Lisht, while still another block probably comes from the Chephren Pyramid Temple. The limestone walls under the colonnade

37

surrounding the court of the Cheops Pyramid Temple were evidently decorated with reliefs. From here probably came our recently acquired block (Fig. 18) which was found by the Metropolitan Museum's Expedition at Lisht where it had been taken by Amenemhat I at the beginning of Dynasty XII, to be reused in construction at his pyramid. It bears the Golden Horus Name of Cheops, whose figure once appeared under the protecting wings of the Horus Falcon on the right. This adjoined a procession of personified royal estates, one of the groups which followed the emblem of each province of the country which brought offerings of its produce to the king. A second block from Lisht with running bowmen of the king's bodyguard (Fig. 16) also came from an Old Kingdom royal temple but since similar archers appear in the Saqqarah Pyramid Temple of Weserkaf, the first king of Dynasty V, it is not certain that this came from Giza. The superlatively fine cutting of these low reliefs disappears after the reign of Sahura but it is now evident that the well-known examples of temple decoration in Dynasty V were anticipated at Giza in Dynasty IV. Such decoration is paralleled by the very fragmentary but beautiful wall scenes in this collection from the pyramid chapel of one of Cheops' queens and provides a logical precedent for the use of reliefs in private tombs. The 1951-1952 excavations in the Valley Temple of Sneferu's Southern Pyramid at Dahshur have also produced a wonderful series of reliefs of the beginning of Dynasty IV which had been anticipated by the fragments of Dynasties II-III at Hierakonpolis, Gebelein, and Heliopolis.

While the exceptional delicacy of modelling of the Cheops low reliefs continued into the reign of Chephren in the chapels of Merytyetes III (G. 7650) and Ankh-haf (G 7510), the majority of the chapels were carved in relief of medium height that lacks superlatively smooth finish of surface. The reliefs of Nofer of the time of Chephren (Fig. 15) vary considerably in quality, while the door-jamb of Kanofer (No. 34.57), toward the end of the dynasty, is characteristic of the relief of medium height which is found in most of the chapels of the Eastern Cemetery.

A high, bold type of relief is also found at Giza in Dynasty IV. A good example of this is the head of a man (No. 34.60) which may come from the chapel of the wife of Khufu-khaf. The reliefs of Khufu-khaf represent this style of carving at its best, while the chapel is the most completely preserved of the early simple offering rooms still *in situ* in the cemetery. Bold relief was imitated in the chapels of lesser persons, as in the wall from the offering room of Sennu-ka (No. 07.-1000) and that from the mastaba G 2175 (No. 12.1512). Sennu-ka is probably the same man as the scribe shown on the door-jamb of Nofer, beside whose tomb he built his own toward the end of Dynasty IV. The reliefs are unfinished, with traces of the preliminary sketch lines and the first stages of the cutting. Another technique, in which the figures and hieroglyphs are sunk beneath the surface of the stone, began to be employed extensively about the time of Chephren. The big false-door of Khufu-ankh is decorated entirely in this sunk relief (No. 21.3081). This fine stela was presented to Khufu-ankh by the king, as we learn from the

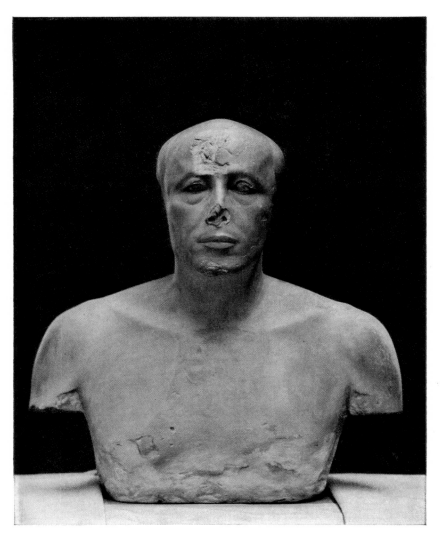

17. Painted limestone bust of Prince Ankh-haf

18. Relief probably from temple of Great Pyramid at Giza (detail)

inscriptions. Probably the royal donor was Weserkaf, the first king of Dynasty V, whose name appeared on a jar-sealing found in the burial chamber of the tomb.

While the offering room of the Dynasty IV chapel was decorated with simple scenes showing the owner seated at his funerary meal and, often accompanied by his family, receiving the offerings of food and personal equipment for his tomb, the external stone rooms of the more elaborate chapels of the royal princes in the Eastern Cemetery provided space for a variety of wall scenes. These tombs have been thoroughly plundered for their fine stone, but enough fragments remain to show that there were scenes from life such as had occurred already in the tombs at Medum. One of these, from a swamp scene in the chapel of the Crown Prince Ka-wab (Fig. 19), shows us a man, perhaps the prince himself, leaning on his staff in a boat. Behind him a tame heron, probably used as a decoy, stands on a crate filled with ducks. The rock-cut tombs prepared for the family of Chephren provided even greater wall space for the expansion of these scenes from life. The range of subject matter familiar from the Dynasty V chapels at Saqqarah is found almost complete in the wonderfully preserved painted reliefs of Meresankh III. This rock-cut tomb, found by the Museum's Expedition, is probably to be dated to the reign of Shepseskaf at the end of Dynasty IV.

Although the destruction of his pyramid temple and the disappearance of the valley temple under the modern village has deprived us of statues of Cheops, we

41

are amply compensated by the sculpture from the temples of other kings of Dynasty IV. From the reign of Cheops' successor, Radedef, a wonderful head of the king in the Louvre and some other fragmentary pieces in Cairo have survived. Chephren has not only left us his portrait in the great Sphinx of Giza, the most ambitious work of sculpture in the Old Kingdom, but also the famous diorite seated statue in Cairo, found by Mariette in the granite valley temple beside the Sphinx. In the plundering of Chephren's pyramid temple many statues were dragged over into the Western Cemetery, where a workshop was set up to manufacture small alabaster vessels for the tombs of the later Old Kingdom. Of several heads which have escaped this barbarously wasteful process, by far the finest is the delicately carved alabaster face of Chephren shown in Fig. 21. Terribly battered, but even more beautiful in workmanship, is the head No. 34.52, while we possess several other incomplete fragments of royal statues.

The red painted limestone bust of Prince Ankh-haf (Fig. 17) was found in a room in the exterior brick chapel of an enormous mastaba in the Eastern Cemetery which was probably built in the reign of Chephren. Ankh-haf was the eldest son of a king and as Vizier and Overseer of all the King's Works he was one of the most important men of the time, a fact fully borne out by the size of his tomb. This is only exceeded by that of the great mastaba G 2000 in the Western Cemetery which probably belonged to a vizier of Cheops' time. It would appear that Ankh-haf was a son of Sneferu, who used the title of ' Eldest Son ' only after the death of Cheops. He would therefore have been Chephren's uncle. Certainly he was able to employ one of the greatest of the royal sculptors.

The portrait of Ankh-haf is unusual in form, resembling a modern bust. The upper part of the torso is finished off at about the middle of the chest with a flat surface underneath upon which the piece can stand, while the arms are cut off a little below the shoulders. Nothing else quite like this is known, although in two other cases the upper part of a figure has been carved within the architectural frame of the false-door of a tomb. It is quite certain that the Ankh-haf bust was a free-standing piece. It was found overturned in front of a low brick bench in one of the chapel rooms and probably stood originally on this bench, even though this seems an inadequate support for such an important piece. Although it is difficult to detect under the painted surface, a coat of plaster, varying in depth, was laid down over the limestone and some of the finer details are carved in this plaster layer. The missing short beard was probably made entirely of plaster. The base where it was broken off is just visible. The missing ears were probably carved in stone. Traces of the use of plaster to fill out mistakes in cutting and as a final surface are to be found in some of the reserve heads, but to what extent this was employed it is difficult to determine.

The plastic treatment of the planes of the face has extended a great deal further here than in the reserve heads. The modelling of the eyes, with the suggestion of pouches beneath, and the realistic treatment of eyelids and brow, as well as the bunching of the muscles at the corner of the mouth, are remarkable. The same subtlety of modelling is to be observed, however, both in the Louvre head of Radedef, which incidentally bears a remarkable facial resemblance to Ankhhaf, and in the head of our large alabaster seated figure of Mycerinus (Fig. 24). It is in the plastic use of minor surface planes in these three heads that we find the clearest means of recognizing a school of sculptors different from that which employed a simplified, broader modelling as in the reserve heads, the seated Chephren in Cairo, or the slate pair of Mycerinus and his queen (Fig. 22). That this was not entirely a question of the realistic intent of the sculptor can be seen by comparing the knee structure of the alabaster Mycerinus with the modelling on the body of the Hildesheim statue of Hemiunu. No one could deny the naturalistic effect of the rolls of fat on the torso of Hemiunu, but the treatment is in broad simple masses without the subtlety of modelling and carefully worked detail of the Mycerinus statue.

In the sculpture from the pyramid temples of Mycerinus we find both groups working with the same aims in view but each following its own technical tradition. It is perhaps because a larger number of statues escaped destruction than from any preceding reign that the range in types is wider, giving us examples of the simple grouping of figures which were to form classic models throughout the history of Egyptian sculpture. Thus in the slate pair, Queen Kha-merer-nebty stands beside her husband, placing one arm around his waist while her other arm rests upon his arm (Fig. 22). One feels in this statue, as in the other great pieces of Dynasty IV, that the ideal of kingly majesty has been achieved. Everything superficial has been eliminated. Details of dress and decoration have been subordinated to the imposing form of the royal figures. Although the modelling is superb and the statue had been painted, the final stages of carving had not been entirely completed, probably because of the king's sudden death. The heads have received their final polish, but the lower part of the figures is still rough and the base was never inscribed.

The various stages in the working of these hard stone statues can be seen in a series of diorite statuettes which were left incomplete at the king's death. We can follow the work through the first steps of blocking out the figure with the aid of red guiding lines to the point where the master took over the cutting of the finer modelling and the polishing of the surfaces. The figure was shaped by abrasion with stone implements, while rubbing stones served for the polishing. Some sort of grinding paste, probably quartz sand, was needed to make the copper tools effective. Marks can be found on hard stone statues to prove the use of a copper saw, a hollow boring tube, and drills of copper or stone.

The slate triad from the Mycerinus valley temple (Fig. 23) was completely finished. Except that it has lost most of its color, it is in an amazingly perfect state of preservation. The Goddess Hathor sits in the center, between a standing figure of the king and a personification of the Hare Nome. The inscription on the base gives the speech of Hathor: " I have given to you all good offerings of the South forever," which means that the Nome figure in this statue served the same

19. Prince Ka-wab in his boat after trapping birds

20. The Vizier Hemiunu

21. Alabaster face of King Chephren

purpose as did the personifications of estates bearing food offerings on the walls of the private tombs. The Hare Nome lay in Upper Egypt. Its capital was the important city of Hermopolis to which the Middle Kingdom tombs of Bersheh belonged. It was in this district that Akhenaten later built his new capital at Tell el Amarna. Three other triads found with this also represented provinces of Upper Egypt, and it is not unlikely that there were originally statues representing all the Nomes of Upper and Lower Egypt. Through these the king would have been able to draw upon the whole country for nourishment after death.

The alabaster seated figure of Mycerinus (Fig. 24) is one of the masterpieces of the new school, with its more plastic treatment of the surfaces. Considerably over life size, it is the best preserved of the colossal statues of the Old Kingdom. In spite of the fame of the Great Sphinx of Giza, there has been a curious tendency to overlook the fact that the sculptors of this period created large works to rival those of Dynasty XVIII. From Dynasty III a few fragments are preserved in Cairo of what must have been a very large statue of Zoser, while a battered limestone statue, also in Cairo, of Queen Kha-merer-nebty I is about the same size as our alabaster figure of her son Mycerinus. The granite head of Weserkaf in the Cairo Museum is all that is preserved of a statue that must have been at least twice the size of these.

Affording a complete contrast to the alabaster colossus, the ivory statuette of Mycerinus is no less a great work of art. Belonging to a very rare class of objects represented only by the tiny ivory Cheops in Cairo and a few other pieces of early date, this figure is a precious possession of the Museum. Although it lacks head, arms, and one leg it still claims attention by its vitality and delicate modelling (Fig. 25).

The youthful-looking head of alabaster (Fig. 27) has been thought to be a portrait of Shepseskaf, the son who succeeded Mycerinus on the throne and completed, albeit with cheaper materials, the work on the pyramid temples left unfinished at his father's death. It was found in the valley temple with the other sculpture of Mycerinus and there is the alternate possibility that it represents that king at an earlier age than in his other portraits. The facial characteristics are similar and the sensitive modelling akin to that of the large alabaster seated figure. Certainly representing one of the sons of the builder of the Third Pyramid is the small yellow limestone scribe (Fig. 26). This was found in the tomb of Khunera, the eldest son of the king, in the quarry cemetery southeast of the pyramid. On one of the chapel walls Khunera is shown as a small naked boy standing beside the throne of his mother Kha-merer-nebty II, who appears in our slate pair. Since the prince never came to the throne, he must have died as a young man, before his father. The broad, plump-cheeked face reminds one of the features of his mother in the slate pair. The pose is one of the early representations of the squatting scribe, known also from statues of Prince Ka-wab (No. 27.1127) and the sons of Radedef (in the Louvre and at Cairo). Although the face is polished the rest of the statue looks as though it lacked the finishing touches.

22. Slate group of King Mycerinus and his Queen

23. The seated Goddess Hathor, King Mycerinus, and the personified
Hare Nome (a province in Upper Egypt)

24. Colossal alabaster statue of Mycerinus

25. Ivory figurine of Mycerinus

26. Khunera, the son of Mycerinus, as a scribe

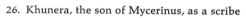

27. Alabaster royal head, probably King Shepseskaf

One of the most interesting members of the royal family of Dynasty IV was Queen Hetep-heres II, a daughter of Cheops. An unusual limestone statuette of this lady and her daughter, Meresankh III, has been put together from fragments found in the rock-cut tomb of the daughter (No. 30.1456). Hetep-heres, who is shown with a yellow wig, a purposeful face, and a gown of unusual cut on a wall of her daughter's tomb, had an extraordinary career. She was the wife of the Crown Prince Ka-wab who was supplanted and perhaps murdered by Radedef. The latter married the widowed Hetep-heres, but she survived his short reign and allied herself to the faction that returned to power by marrying her daughter to the new king Chephren. Behind these brief facts must lie a bitter tale of court intrigue and jealousies within the harîm.

In the chapel of Meresankh were found the earliest known limestone statuettes of men and women cooking and slaughtering animals. These so-called servant figures were to become common in the statue chambers of Dynasty V. The Meresankh statuettes had been badly smashed, but three fragmentary figures survived which are in this collection (No. 30.1458).

DYNASTY V TO DYNASTY VI

In Dynasty V the large number of craftsmen trained in the vast undertakings of the kings of Dynasty IV made it possible for the average man of moderate wealth to own a statue of tolerably good quality. At the same time the use of wall reliefs expanded greatly. In the large tombs the walls of room after room were covered with reliefs, while even the small chapels were decorated with wall scenes. The effects of this expanding activity extended beyond the cemeteries attached to the capital. Small statues were shipped to Upper Egypt and a few of the provincial nobles at such places as Tehneh, Hemamieh, and Sheikh Said were able to have their rock-cut tombs decorated with reliefs. Although this was to extend further in Dynasty VI, it was by no means the general practice in Dynasty V, as is shown by the miserably crude stelae with which the people buried in the cemetery at Naga-ed-Dêr had to be content.

Technical proficiency now enabled the royal architects to replace heavy pillars and piers with granite supports fashioned into plant forms – palm and bundle-columns of papyrus and lotus flowers. At the same time plain granite walls were replaced by surfaces covered with painted reliefs. This lent a lighter and more pleasing effect to the temple halls and courts. However, the recovery of fragments of Dynasty IV reliefs from Lisht and Dahshur and from the pyramid temple of Cheops now makes it clear that we cannot judge the appearance of the earlier temples entirely from the severe granite surfaces of the Chephren valley temple. Hitherto unsuspected elements of decoration have disappeared in the destruction of the temples of Sneferu, Cheops, and Chephren. Moreover, the superb quality of these royal fragments makes it apparent that in Dynasty V it was only the sculptors of Weserkaf and Sahura who maintained the same high standard, although it was regained briefly in the temple of Pepy II in Dynasty VI. We must not forget in the presence of the exuberant variety and quantity of the private reliefs of Dynasty V that they seldom approach in technical skill such masterpieces of the preceding period as the chapels of Khufu-khaf, Hemiunu, Mery-tyetes, and Ankh-haf. Like the royal reliefs, all of these, with the exception of the chapel of Khufu-khaf, are in such a fragmentary condition that it is not surprising that they have remained relatively unnoticed. Nevertheless they show us that Dynasty IV was the real period of achievement.

The turn of Dynasty IV to Dynasty V is characterized at Saqqarah by the appearance of a number of large statues of fine quality which are among the most famous of Egyptian works of art. These include such pieces as the Louvre scribe, the statues of Ranofer, and the well-known wooden 'Sheikh el Beled' in Cairo. At Giza was found a series of statues rivalling these in quality. Although, from the time that Shepseskaf built his tomb at Saqqarah South, the kings of Egypt were no longer buried at Giza, a number of important people who were related to the old families, or who served as funerary priests of the royal house of Dynasty IV, continued to build their tombs in the old necropolis. From one of these tombs, dated by a jar sealing to the reign of Shepseskaf, comes the splendid head of red granite (Fig. 28). This impressive portrait of Seshem-nofer was broken from a statue which formed part of a rich tomb equipment. A panelled statue chamber of unusual form was decorated with excellent reliefs, as was the inner

28. Red granite head of Seshem-
    nofer

offering room. A beautifully worked granite sarcophagus contained the burial. Seshem-nofer was head of the Department of Public Works, while his son, continuing in this office, became the vizier of one of the first kings of Dynasty V.

The elaborate provision made for the statues of Seshem-nofer is paralleled by the large serdabs of Ba-baf which formed separate architectural units attached to his tomb. From the smashed contents of these statue chambers it has been estimated that they contained as many as fifty statues of various materials. One of the most attractive of these is an alabaster statuette pieced together from many small fragments (No. 24.603). The other hard stone statues were almost all irretrievably smashed, but one small granite head was preserved (No. 21.950), and a black granite seated scribe is practically complete (No. 21.931). There were at least ten nearly life-size standing statues of white limestone. These have all lost their heads, but the modelling of the bodies is of the finest quality. To appreciate this one has only to look at the somewhat later statues of Pen-meru (No. 12. 1504) where the modelling has become simple and schematized, particularly in the sharply marked line at the base of the breast muscles. The same simplification and broad, rather coarse treatment can be seen in the famous Cairo statue of Thiy from the close of the dynasty, if this is compared with the more detailed modelling of the Saqqarah statues of Ranofer in Cairo which are contemporary with those of Ba-baf.

The statues of Pen-meru are probably to be dated to about the middle of Dynasty V. In his tiny chapel was inscribed a will referring to the Vizier Seshem-nofer mentioned above, which would probably make Pen-meru a somewhat younger contemporary of that great man. Both pieces of sculpture are what Professor Capart has called a pseudo-group, that is, several figures all representing the same man. It is hard to say whether this curious custom was thought of as

53

29. Detail of family group of Pen-meru

showing the man in different aspects according to the offices that he held, or simply designed to provide another substitute in case any of the figures was injured. In both Pen-meru groups the man is dressed in the same short skirt, but in that showing the three male figures alone (No. 12.1504) the wigs have been differentiated. In the other statue (Fig. 29), two figures of Pen-meru are accompanied by his wife and two children. The statues have been carved inside a frame with a round moulding and architrave above, inscribed with an offering formula and the owner's titles and name. The triad of Pen-meru has not only the schematic modelling of the breast muscles, but a harsher use of simplified planes in the face which anticipates similar features in the style of Dynasty VI. The facial modelling of the wooden statue of Senezem-ib Mehy (Fig. 30) and that of the seated limestone statue of Akh-merut-nesut (No. 12.1482) are closely related.

Although large statues of stone are rare after the first half of Dynasty V, they continued to be made in wood. The chances against the preservation of a wooden statue are so great that we are doubly fortunate in having two of such fine quality as those of Mehy (Fig. 30) and Methethy (Fig. 31). The Methethy statue came from Saqqarah and follows the old Fourth Dynasty treatment of the rounded forms of the face. Other statues of this same man in Brooklyn and Kansas City depart even more markedly from this traditional treatment than does the new style of Mehy's statue. A similar change is to be felt in the bolder cutting on a block of painted relief (Frontispiece) which also belongs to this time of transition at the turn of Dynasty V to Dynasty VI. Naked figures of large size were seldom made and the modelling of the body is exceptionally fine in the case of Mehy who belonged to the important Senezem-ib family whose members were architects and Overseers of all the King's Works over a long period of time down to the end of Dynasty VI. They included Nekhebu, whose statuettes and reliefs will be discussed presently (Fig. 36), and Impy, whose intact burial was one of the latest additions to the family tomb complex (Fig. 38). Mehy lived in the reign of Isesy,

30. Wooden statue of Mehy

as we learn from a biographical inscription in the tomb of his father, Senezem-ib Yenty, which Mehy himself completed for him. Mehy became the vizier of Unas, the last king of Dynasty V. In his burial chamber were some curious little wooden figures of bound prisoners (Nos. 13.3458, 9). They apparently imitate larger stone figures of captives that stood in the temples of kings, but what purpose they can have served here in a private tomb is obscure.

The statues of the second half of Dynasty V are mostly small, ranging from tiny statuettes to figures about one-half life-size. They were moderately well worked and represent a surprisingly high level of skill, considering the quantities of them that were produced. They were really just the stock in trade of the undertakers, like the wooden coffins, offering tables, model vessels, and other tomb equipment. We possess a large number of these statues from the Expedition's work at Giza, a few of which are outstanding in quality. Such is the attractive yellow limestone bust broken from a seated figure (No. 30.830), or the painted statue of Ptah-khenuwy and his wife, with the color almost as fresh as on the day when it was placed in the statue chamber (Fig. 32). The tombs from which these statues came were built in the streets between the royal mastabas and along the edges of the older cemetery at Giza, while at Saqqarah similarly crowded conditions existed, forcing a greater irregularity in the plans of the tombs. Each mastaba contained at least one serdab, or closed statue chamber. Usually this was placed behind the offering niche of the chapel and frequently a small slit was cut through the niche so that the fumes of the funerary priest's censer could reach the statue. In the serdab, the statues of the owner and his wife were frequently accompanied by figures of their children and by servant statuettes. We have a complete group of this sort from the tomb of a man named Wery (Nos. 21.2595-2601). In addition to several statues of the man and his wife and a pair statue of their son and his wife, there was a kneeling woman grinding corn and another tending a fire. From another intact group (Fig. 33) comes the attractive little naked boy (No. 06.1881), and a triad of male figures (No. 06.1882).

The wall decorations of Dynasty V are excellently illustrated by two chapels excavated by Mariette at Saqqarah. That of Ptah-sekhem-ankh (No. 04.1760) consisted of a long offering room set at right angles to an undecorated entrance corridor. The false-door occupied the west wall at the end of the room. It was intended to form the magical means of passage to and from the burial chamber. On the panels of this door are inscribed prayers to the god of the dead and the titles and name of the owner. In the tablet over the central niche, Ptah-sekhem-ankh is shown seated before a table of bread at his funerary meal. This scene is represented on a larger scale on the adjoining wall, with the addition of a great offering list, accompanied by men bringing food and slaughtering oxen for the meal (Fig. 34). These pictures were designed to provide Ptah-sekhem-ankh with an inexhaustible supply of food, as well as furnishing the texts to be recited by his funerary priests to make this food available to him in spirit form.

In Dynasty V, scenes from life, which further amplified this food supply by

31. Wooden statue of Methethy

representing the source from which it came, began to be included in the inner offering room. These lively pictures are of the greatest interest to us, for from them can be reconstructed most of what we know about the daily life of the Old Kingdom. The scenes in this chapel are restricted to the elements most important to the Egyptian: the cultivation of the land, the raising of cattle, and the various pursuits undertaken in the swamp lands. The composition of the wall is built up from groups of figures each engaged in a characteristic action. These are combined in long superimposed registers each beginning in front of the large figure of the owner which dominates the wall. Usually the progression is from the upper register downwards, but sometimes the individual groups are arbitrarily combined. Thus in the cultivation of Ptah-sekhem-ankh's farm the men plowing should precede, not follow, the sower, while the flax harvest is interpolated between the plowing and the cutting of the barley. Similarly, the different scenes on the same wall are not always related in subject matter. In this case we have a register of desert animals, then a group of fighting boatmen and a partially destroyed bird-trapping scene, followed by the cultivation of barley and flax. The register system was used not only to represent the continuity of action, but, to a

Opposite: 32. Statuette of Ptah-khenuwy and his wife

33. Serdab with statuettes of Bau and his family

lesser extent, to show things which existed in different visual planes. That is, objects near at hand would be placed in the lowest register while those farther away in the distance would be in the register above. This was employed only within a limited area and never extended logically throughout the whole wall surface. A good example of this on the same wall of Ptah-sekhem-ankh is the sub-register which shows a hare and a small hyena above, instead of beyond, the procession of desert animals in the top register, or the two seated men with crates of birds in the second register which should be side by side instead of one above the other. Once we have grasped the principle of representation, these pictures express themselves clearly enough.

In front of the figure of Ptah-sekhem-ankh surveying the work on his estate is a line of inscription which sums up the important action: ' Seeing the work of the fields, the plowing, cutting of barley, and pulling of flax, loading the donkeys and driving the donkeys, the winnowing on the threshing floor.' Unmentioned are the two upper registers where the desert animals, which include a rare picture of a stag, can be thought of as a kind of short-hand representation of the hunting scene for which there was no room. By showing the results of the chase the whole subject is suggested, and Ptah-sekhem-ankh can receive its benefits equally well. Similarly abbreviated are the swamp activities which have overlapped from the adjoining wall, where a papyrus thicket and the breeding and care of cattle in the Delta marshes are shown. A missing block has obliterated the bird trap, which a group of men are about to close by pulling on a cord at the signal of their comrade who waves a scarf. To the right of them appears a mock combat between men garlanded with lotus flowers, who joust with long poles from light papyrus canoes.

The complete agricultural cycle is shown on this wall. The sower is followed by a herd of sheep to trample the grain into the plowed ground. As suggested above, the ox-drawn plows should precede this group. Over the destroyed sheep was written a favorite song of the shepherd, known from other chapels. Only a word or two remains here, but it is addressed to the fish in the ponds, implying that the shepherd in his swampy solitude had no other companions. In the next row, on the right, men pull up flax (almost entirely destroyed) and tie it into bundles, while on the left peasants cut the barley with sickles. This is piled into hampers, and in the next register we see them loaded on the backs of donkeys to be carried to the threshing floor. In the lowest register men stack the bundles beside the threshing floor, where donkeys are driven round and round in a circle to trample out the grain. A baby donkey stands on the edge of the threshing floor. The straw is then forked up into a stack, while women winnow the chaff with flat wooden scoops. Finally, on the right, a man measures out the grain in the pile for the scribes to record.

On the narrow adjoining wall the artist has varied his pictures of the raising of cattle by a number of individual touches. Note, for instance, the fat man squatting down to assist at the birth of a calf, or the overseer comfortably ensconced

34. Butchering scene in chapel of Ptah-sekhem-ankh

in a light shelter with a supply of provisions, while a man offers him a drink. The calves sketched in with lightly incised lines may owe part of their look of movement to re-drawing, but they give an unusually lively impression. The cow drinking from a basin below has a label saying ' drink for the cow.'

The reliefs of the chapel of Ka-em-nofret (No. 04.1761) are similar to those just described. The room had a different shape. It was entered from the middle of the east wall and had a large, beautifully inscribed false-door in the center of the opposite wall. Again a swamp scene occupies the narrow end wall (Fig. 35). The birds flying above the papyrus thicket are so carefully drawn that it is easy to recognize the different species: hoopoe, egret, kingfisher, lapwing, heron, ibis, cormorant, and pigeon. Men are shown pulling the papyrus and tying it into bundles as well as making mats and twisting rope. The lower part of the wall has been altered anciently. A boat-building scene was obliterated in order to add a large figure of Ka-em-nofret hunting birds from a canoe. The wall at the other end of the chapel has been badly damaged but originally contained a carrying-chair scene beneath a large figure of the owner. A dwarf with a monkey accompanies the carrying-chair. The offering scenes have been reduced to the lowest registers of the walls where a few men are shown carrying food, while the offering list itself is represented in the narrow space on each side of the false-door. There was no space for the table scene except on the tablet of the false-door.

The entrance wall is devoted to scenes from life which resemble those of Ptah-sekhem-ankh, but with the addition of a group of men pulling in a large net filled with fish. The stone of the lower part of the wall is of bad quality throughout the chapel and here, where the color is almost all gone, it requires close examination to recognize the subject matter of the scenes. Above, on the right, amongst men

35. Activities of the papyrus marshes, chapel of Ka-em-nofret

tying up bundles of flax, is a remarkable piece of foreshortening in the drawing of a squatting figure shown in front view. Rare as are such figures, we have another example in the standing figure in the inner niche of the little false-door of Redynes (No. 21.961). In this case the face and the body are drawn in front view but the feet are turned out to the sides. The figure is really a cheap imitation of those false-doors which have a statue of the owner standing in the inner niche as though issuing from the tomb.

Although much of the sculpture in relief of Dynasty VI is indistinguishable from that of the preceding period a high, bolder type of carving began to appear toward the end of Dynasty V which is in marked contrast to the very low reliefs that had been prevalent until then. The new style appears in the painted relief of a man named Mehu from a scene on his Giza chapel wall where he was shown spearing fish in the marshes (Frontispiece). In the first reign of Dynasty VI the style was further developed at Saqqarah in the tombs of the courtiers around the pyramid of King Tety. It found its finest expression toward the end of the Dynasty in the wonderful wall decorations of the temple of Pepy II. Other reliefs of Dynasty VI, like those of Nekhebu at Giza, are low and follow the tradition of Dynasty V. Nekhebu's wall scenes are not especially well cut and are chiefly interesting for the variety of subject matter and the liveliness in the movement of the figures. Note, for example, the man who hangs down from the rigging of a ship in the relief No. 13.4349. Nekhebu was a descendant of the Senezem-ib family at Giza and has left a biography (No. 13.4331) dated to the reign of Pepy I, which is like that of his architect ancestor, Senezem-ib Yenty. His tomb belonged to a family group and contained a peculiar serdab which had rows of statues painted on its walls. A block from this serdab is that numbered 13.4339.

The statuettes of Nekhebu are quite unlike the majority of the small pieces of sculpture of Dynasty VI, which ordinarily resemble Dynasty V types. The facial structure and schematized modelling, of which there was a hint in the statues of Pen-meru and Mehy, are further developed here. The impression produced by these little figures is one of deliberate stylization rather than inferior craftsmanship. There is an unusually plastic quality to the haggard face and the torso modelling of the badly damaged small seated figure (No. 13.3149)(Fig. 36) which still exists in the simplified surfaces of the other figures and heads. This became dry and angular in the statuettes at the end of the Old Kingdom, when the failing abilities of the artists resulted in what was almost a caricature of the style of the Nekhebu sculpture. This is plainly evident in the yellow limestone seated figure of Thetety from Saqqarah (No. 24.605).

The decline in craftsmanship at the end of the Old Kingdom is vividly illustrated by a portion of a small offering niche from Saqqarah (No. 24.594). The drawing of the figures bringing food offerings and slaughtering a bull is fairly competent but the relief is cut in one plane with a sharp edge to the outlines. The poverty of the period caused the reduction of the scenes formerly covering the walls of an entire chapel to a few abbreviated groups of figures on a small stone.

36. Statuette of Nekhebu

This example retains a fair approximation of the Memphite style as it was carried on into the First Intermediate Period after the end of Dynasty VI but we can also see that something new was developing in the provinces of Upper Egypt. This is apparent in the crude carvings on the tombstones from the Naga-ed-Dêr district or the very similar stela thought to come from Gebelein south of Thebes, which shows the owner with his household and a pair of dogs (Fig. 47). While the clumsy drawing and harsh colors of these stelae reveal the collapse of technical skill in Upper Egypt, there is a crude vigor here which also appears in the remarkable paintings on a wooden coffin (Fig. 48) and which points to the revival that was to come in the Middle Kingdom.

The burial equipment recovered from the tombs of the Old Kingdom rounds out a picture of the life of the early Egyptians which is perhaps more complete than that of any other ancient people. The favorite members of the Cheops family were buried in large granite coffins of which that of Queen Meresankh II of Dynasty IV is a fine example (No. 27.441). The outer faces are decorated with a complicated series of niches and panels which imitated the great gate of the king's palace, and were designed to permit the dead person easy passage to and from his coffin. On the lid is the large jackal figure of Anubis, the god of the dead, forming part of a prayer addressed to him and at the same time serving as a guardian genius for the person buried inside. On the ends of the coffin are granaries and a short offering list. Less wealthy people had to be content with wooden coffins which came to be used more and more by important people after Dynasty IV, as in the case of Impy, the last important descendant of the Senezem-ib family, whose coffin (No. 13.3085) was found in an intact tomb of Dynasty VI. By this time the coffins bore simple bands of text containing, in addition to the titles and name of the owner, a prayer for a good burial addressed to Osiris as well as Anubis. On one side of the coffin was inscribed a pair of eyes opposite the place where the face of the dead man lay, in order to permit him to see what was going on in the outer world.

The body was wrapped elaborately in linen which usually simulated the form and even the dress of the dead person. The moulded wrappings of the face were sometimes painted to add to the naturalism of the simulacrum. It was evidently felt that a more permanent form should be given to these perishable wrappings, and it is very probable that the limestone reserve heads were placed in the burial chambers of Dynasty IV to serve as a substitute for the head. Often the head, and sometimes even the whole body, was cased in plaster which seems to have suggested the mummy masks of the First Intermediate Period and the cartonnage cases of the Middle Kingdom. Several of these masks, modelled over the linen wrappings of the face of the mummy, have a decided value as portraits (Nos. 37.644, 39.828) (Fig. 37). The head of the mummy was placed on a headrest with a curved upper support fastened to a stem, usually fluted, set in a rectangular base. The finer examples were often made of alabaster, like No. 21. 2790, which belonged to the same Khufu-ankh whose stela is mentioned on p. 38, but limestone examples are frequently found, and some of the wooden pieces are beautifully made (No. 37.1332).

37. Plaster mask from a mummy

38. Intact burial chamber of Impy when first opened

39. Gold collar of Impy

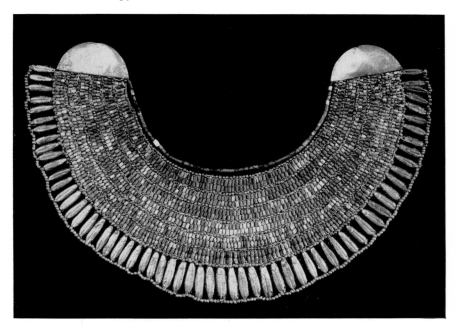

On the body was placed a set of jewelry consisting usually of a broad neck-lace, bracelets, and anklets. The finest of these broad collars came from the coffin of Impy mentioned on p. 64. It was composed of hundreds of little gold-covered ring and barrel heads (Fig. 39). Similar necklaces made of blue faience are also exhibited with the bracelets which accompanied them (No. 37.1314). One neck-lace has a counterpoise such as we sometimes see painted at the back of the neck on statues (Nos. 37.1311-1313). It was intended to balance the weight of the heavy collar. Women seem to have worn bead-net garments, as in life, although none has been preserved intact. A mass of beads scattered over a burial may have come from such a net, since there were also gold covered copper pendants which seem to have hung from the hem of the garment. From this same burial came a copper crown covered with gold leaf laid on a plaster coating. Around the band are set large rosettes, formed of papyrus umbels with birds and hieroglyphic em-blems, made of painted and gilded gesso. In the center of each design is a round carnelian inlay (No. 37.606).

One burial of a woman at Giza had several wooden combs placed in the wrap-pings of the head (No. 37.1322). Although these are found in Predynastic graves, they are exceedingly rare in the Old Kingdom. In the wrappings of another mummy was found a wooden belt buckle imitating the tie at the waist of the skirt so frequently seen in statues and reliefs (No. 37.1317). Another coffin contained a wooden walking stick and a ' sekhem-wand ' laid beside the body (Nos. 37. 1318 and 1323). These symbols of official power appear in the hands of every im-portant man in Old Kingdom representations. From the burials of the Late Old Kingdom and the First Intermediate Period have been recovered other articles of personal equipment much better preserved in the dry sand of the cemeteries of Upper Egypt than at Giza. Staves, shawls, weapons, as well as coffins and small chests, begin to resemble the equipment of the burials of the Middle Kingdom. Such is the pleated shirt from a late Old Kingdom tomb at Naga-ed-Dêr (No. 34. 56).

Of the household equipment placed in the burial chambers at Giza, the plun-derers have seldom left much save broken fragments of the pottery vessels which contained food and drink, or stone vessels and models used for the same purpose. Stone models of different kinds of food were sometimes made and placed in the tomb, such as the little alabaster pieces (No. 21.2818, etc.), while Dynasty VI tombs often contained large limestone cases carved in the shape of trussed birds or pieces of meat, which held the actual food itself (No. 13.3480, etc.). A neces-sary part of the equipment was a magical set like that of Cheops, found in the valley temple of Mycerinus (No. 11.765, etc.). When complete, the vessels were fitted into the depressions of a stone tray like No. 13.3144, and included an in-strument known as the Peseshkaf-wand. This was used in the ceremony of the ' opening of the mouth,' and the whole set served to enable the dead man to par-take of the food supplied to him.

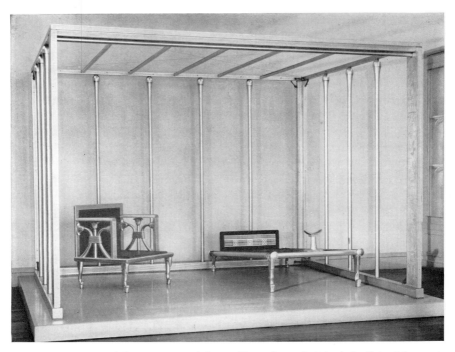

40. Reproductions of the Furniture of Queen Hetep-heres (originals in Cairo Museum)

The large collection of pottery of the Old Kingdom is made particularly interesting by a representative group of vessels from the tomb of Queen Hetep-heres
I, mother of Cheops. Old Kingdom pottery was undecorated and ranged from a
coarse brownish ware to a thin, fine fabric with a red polished surface. Quite different, and certainly foreign in origin, is the buff-colored pottery, often covered
with a light-colored slip and with the surface frequently marked with striated
combings. These vessels are all tall jars with handles on the shoulders, such as
might have contained oil. The handled jug, which sometimes appears, resembles
the Syrian vessels which are shown in the tribute presented to Sahura.

Two important Giza tombs escaped plundering. One of these belonged to the
mother of Cheops at the beginning of Dynasty IV, the other to the previously
mentioned official of Pepy II, Impy, who carried on the Senezem-ib family tradition as Overseer of all the King's Works in Dynasty VI (Fig. 38). The contrast to
be seen between the contents of the two is due to the changes in funerary practices during a considerable length of time rather than to the difference in rank between a Queen Mother and a court architect. The tomb of Impy no longer contains large pieces of furniture such as had been used by the deceased in his own
house during his lifetime. Aside from a few vessels of pottery and copper and the
personal possessions buried in the coffin, most of Impy's equipment consisted of
copper models of offering tables with their accompanying vessels, as well as

many model tools. It is impossible to tell whether the princely mastabas of Dynasty IV contained articles of furniture resembling those of Hetep-heres. If they did, every vestige has disappeared. The chapel reliefs show us that the wealthy houses were furnished with pieces like the armchair, bed, carrying-chair, and bed canopy of Hetep-heres. It may well be that these wall reliefs were thought of as taking the place of the real equipment no longer put in the burial chamber.

The furniture of Hetep-heres (reproductions of the original pieces in the Cairo Museum are exhibited) demonstrates more clearly than anything else the high degree of culture to which the Egyptian nobility had attained in the Old Kingdom (Fig. 40). The luxury of these gold-covered pieces is tempered by severe good taste, which gives them a clean simplicity of line that is lacking in the more flamboyant furniture of the New Kingdom, as created by the cabinetmakers who worked for Tut-ankh-amon. The beauty of the inlaid designs, so effectively expressed in the flower pattern on the footboard of the bed or the inscriptions on the curtain box is found again in the more complex patterns on one of the queen's two arm-chairs and another chest which so far it has only been possible to restore on paper. The hieroglyphic inscriptions on the jambs of the bed canopy, and the tiny gold hieroglyphs set into the ebony panels of the carrying-chair, are unrivalled in design and workmanship. The Museum was accorded fragments of one of the ten pairs of silver bracelets originally mounted in a gold covered box. The lapis lazuli, turquoise and carnelian inlays of two of the butterflies are shown in Fig. 41 with a reproduction of one of the Cairo bracelets.

41. Inlaid bracelet of Queen Hetep-heres
(copy of one in Cairo and original inlays from another)

42. King Mentuhotep II from his Deir el Bahari temple, Dyn. XI

Chapter III

The Middle Kingdom

THE HISTORICAL BACKGROUND

ABOUT THE MIDDLE of the twenty-second century B.C. a wealthy family of princes in Assiut was the chief support of the kings of Dynasty X who ruled at Heracleopolis. Even then the growing strength of the Theban Nome made itself felt in Middle Egypt. Tef-ib, the Nomarch of Assiut, tells us how he fought the Thebans and drove them back in the Thinite region. Probably this is the same fighting that is referred to by Zari, one of the followers of Intef II. The early princes of Thebes seem to have offered some kind of nominal allegiance to Heracleopolis, but the father of this king Intef discarded any semblance of loyalty to the throne in the North and assumed royal titles for himself.

The second king of Dynasty X, Khety III, had managed to drive the Asiatics out of the Delta and to bring Lower Egypt back to a fairly prosperous condition. However, the House of Heracleopolis does not seem to have been very firmly in control of the Memphite region, which had been so wracked by internal strife during Dynasties VIII and IX.

The military strength of Assiut was necessary to establish Khety's son Merikara on the throne. Nevertheless, peaceful relations with the South seem to have been maintained throughout this reign, and we find Tef-ib's son in Assiut able to turn his attention to the improvement of his Nome. There is no account of the final fall of Assiut, but there is perhaps some evidence that the prince of Hermopolis, Nehery, undertook the task of defending the northern kingdom after the Thebans had seized Assiut. The resistance cannot have continued for long. The Southerners who died at the taking of Heracleopolis may actually be represented by the common burial near the Deir el Bahari Temple at Thebes of some sixty soldiers slain in battle. Recent investigation favors the idea that the two kings formerly called Mentuhotep II and III were really the same man who assumed a different titulary after the conquest of Heracleopolis.

This king, Mentuhotep II, stands out as the dominant personality of Dynasty XI. He had a very long reign and built at Thebes the great monument of the period, the funerary temple at Deir el Bahari. His architect created a new and very effective architectural form. This was a terraced structure with colonnades, surmounted by a pyramid set in the midst of a columned hall on the upper level. The plan seems to have had its origin in the cemetery of the princes of the Intef family at Thebes, where the tomb of the ruler was cut in the back wall of a court excavated in the lower slopes of the desert. In front of the tomb chamber was a row of square pillars cut from the solidified gravel, while along the side walls of the court were excavated the tombs of the chief man's followers, each preceded by a row of pillars. Thus the impression gained was that of a long court opening into the hillside and surrounded on three sides by a colonnade. The principal tomb seems to have been marked further by a pyramid of brick which perhaps stood at the back of the court. The Abbott Papyrus refers to the pyramid of Intef II. Although there seems to have been some trace of such pyramids in Mariette's time, these brick structures have now disappeared. The combining of colonnades and pyramid in a terraced construction built of stone was a brilliant conception which later seems to have suggested the form of Hatshepsut's neighboring funerary temple in Dynasty XVIII. Incidentally, a terraced structure is known from the Old Kingdom, in the valley temple of Pepy II. This, however, is scarcely more than the manipulation of the different levels of a landing stage. At the end of the Old Kingdom pottery offering trays were made in the form of a model house with a columned porch. Some of them have barrel-vaulted rooms (Fig. 45) and others an exterior staircase leading to a second story. These suggest that the Dynasty XI tombs may have been developed from house architecture.

Mentuhotep's great task must have been the reorganization of the country's administration. All formidable resistance to the royal house had been crushed, but there may have been occasional minor uprisings. However, the political atmosphere of the Middle Kingdom differs from that of earlier times. The peaceful security of the Old Kingdom was a thing of the past. While the siege scenes in the tombs of Baket and Khety at Beni Hasan probably represent battles in the successfully completed war with the North and were only copied again in the later tombs there, the people of Dynasty XII had not yet forgotten the bitter strife of the preceding dynasty nor the hard times that had preceded it in Dynasties VIII and IX. Warlike equipment was painted on the chapel walls and coffins of the Middle Kingdom nobles, while actual weapons and models are found buried with them. The desire for such protection is in sharp contrast to the peaceful requirements of the Old Kingdom dead and is echoed by the pessimistic note in Middle Kingdom literature.

The reliefs of Mentuhotep's temple have preserved fragments of a battle scene, but in this case the attack seems to have been directed against the Bedouins of the eastern desert. However, in spite of these lingering vestiges of strife, Egypt must have been in a fairly prosperous state in the latter half of the reign of Mentuhotep II. The war with Heracleopolis had been fought only in a limited section of central Egypt and had been a desultory affair with interludes of peace punctuating the periods of fighting. The House of Khety had restored Lower Egypt to a comparatively sound condition, while Upper Egypt had been growing strong under the early kings of Dynasty XI. The king's chief problem was the consolidation of the power of the administration in his own hands, and in this he was not entirely successful. The Middle Kingdom rulers seem never to have recovered the absolute control over the country that their predecessors had maintained in the Old Kingdom. Although the great power of the various provincial princes was broken they still retained a semi-feudal relationship to the king. The Nomarch was allowed to administer the local affairs of his district, for which he was responsible to the king.

We know very little about the administration of the Delta in Dynasty XI, although the letters of a man named Heka-nekht give many details about agricultural conditions there. They show a Theban travelling back and forth from his home in the south to care for the interests of the properties that he owned in the north. In Middle Egypt the power of the princes of Assiut must have been destroyed and no one of importance built a tomb there until Hepzefa gained the favor of Sesostris I. The Nomarchs of the Hare and Oryx Nomes, on the other hand, continued to build imposing tombs at Bersheh and Beni Hasan, as though they had lost nothing by the Theban conquest. In Dynasty XII we find wealthy princes also at Aswan, Qau el Kebir, and Meir. Thus, while favorites of the king were also buried in the court cemeteries, we nevertheless find an emphasis upon that regionalism which had begun to make itself felt towards the end of the Old Kingdom. This is apparent in the decoration of the tombs of different districts where local peculiarities appear, in contrast to the Old Kingdom when there had been only one Memphite style of the court throughout the country.

On foreign relations we have little evidence. An inscription of Mentuhotep II was found at Konosso in Nubia, while on a relief in his Gebelein temple we see him striking down a representative of the Nubians, a Libyan, an Asiatic, and an Egyptian who may represent the Heracleopolitans. The Deir-el-Bahari temple reliefs show fighting with the Bedouin tribes as well as tribute brought by men who look like Nubians. Mentuhotep's successors, Se-ankh-kara and Neb-tawy-ra, sent expeditions to work the Hammamat quarries and to reopen the desert road from Coptos to the Red Sea. Se-ankh-kara also despatched an expedition to Punt after communications had been established along this road to enable the building of a ship on the Red Sea. The man who was in charge of quarrying operations at Hammamat under Neb-tawy-ra was a certain Amenemhat, the king's vizier who bore other great titles. It has been suggested very plausibly that this important man, whose energetic personality speaks eloquently from the inscription that he has left in the quarries, is identical with the founder of Dynasty XII, the Pharaoh Amenemhat I who seized the throne of the declining Mentuhotep family.

Thus about the year 2000 B.C. began the succession of powerful rulers who formed Dynasty XII. Amenemhat adopted three important measures which became the core of the family policy of these kings. First he established a new capital at a place called Ith-tawe, not far south of Memphis, where he could better control Lower Egypt and the Delta. At Lisht nearby he built his tomb, reverting

73

to the old Memphite form of pyramidal structure with accompanying temple and mastabas for his courtiers. His followers continued this custom, building their pyramids at Lisht and Dahshur and at the entrance to the Fayum at Lahun and Hawara. Second he initiated the custom of placing his son beside him on the throne as co-regent. In this he seems to have been influenced by a palace conspiracy which seriously endangered his life, and to which he refers bitterly in the admonitions which he left for the guidance of his son, Sesostris I. Third and last Amenemhat undertook the subjugation of Nubia and the establishment of trading stations farther south than had been attempted by any king before him. It is possible that he was the founder of Inebu-Amenemhat, the fortified trading post at Kerma which is found administered by Hepzefa in the following reign of Sesostris I.

The importance of Nubia for the control of the gold mines which lay in the mountains east of Wady Halfa, and the caravan trade which brought the raw products of the south through the ' Land of Roads ' into Egypt, was fully realized by Amenemhat's successors. The expedition of the year 19 of Amenemhat was followed by the real conquest of the country beyond the Second Cataract in the following reign of Sesostris I, who also commenced the construction of the forts in the region of the First and Second Cataracts. Amenemhat II and Sesostris II apparently devoted little time to Nubian affairs, but their successor, Sesostris III, made no less than four campaigns in the south. He also strengthened the system of fortifications by building new forts at Semna, on the island of Uronarti, and at Mirgissa. The very considerable remains of these buildings have, like Kerma, been excavated by the Museum's Expedition, revealing many interesting details of their construction and the life of the frontier garrisons.

In the reign of Sesostris I, Prince Hepzefa was established as governor of Kerma, perhaps succeeding Sa-renput of Aswan. He brought with him from his native Assiut his entire household which included artists and craftsmen of every sort. Thus, far up in the Sudan, was duplicated the life of the self-contained estate of a wealthy noble in Egypt proper. But in Nubia the materials available to the craftsman were different from those to which he had been accustomed at home, requiring certain modifications of technique, while he was at the same time exposed to the influence of the native African crafts. The skill and adaptability of the Egyptian workman asserted themselves under these new conditions. The arrival of these new craftsmen must have acted also as a considerable stimulus to the local industries. The result was the growth of a school of arts and crafts having its own peculiar style which continued to make itself felt, although gradually submerged by native influence, until the more thorough Egyptianization of Nubia during the New Kingdom.

The sculptors brought to Inebu-Amenemhat were certainly good ones and they made such fine statues as that of Hepzefa's wife Sennuwy, using local stone. Hepzefa seems to have been particularly fortunate in his choice of artists, for his tomb at Assiut is decorated with extremely fine, although hopelessly damaged, paintings. While the sculptors continued along traditional lines, the other crafts-men were more powerfully influenced by their surroundings. It is difficult to determine how much the native craftsmen contributed to the Kerma industries. One suspects that in the case of the pottery a local product was developed into a new ware of unusual thinness and fine polish which somewhat resembles the black-topped red ware of the Predynastic Period but is finer in quality and more interesting in shape. The makers of weapons produced fine copper daggers with elaborate pommels of ivory, different in shape from those used in Egypt, while the furniture makers employed ivory inlays of local animals with certain new elements introduced into the design. Similar animal and plant forms were cut from mica and applied to caps and clothing. Even the makers of faience, a purely Egyptian industry, created plastic forms in the shape of tiles and sculptured re-vetments which have not been found elsewhere, while at the same time produc-ing blue-glazed bowls with charming patterns of birds and animals such as are known from Egypt itself. Unfortunately the wall paintings in two of the chapels were badly preserved. They were crudely executed and bear little resemblance to the careful draughtsmanship of Dynasty XII paintings. What remains consists chiefly of pictures of giraffes, hippopotami, and boats, but the style contains no element that can be identified as local. They are probably to be dated to the Sec-ond Intermediate Period when similarly crude work was being done in Egypt, for example in the tombs at El Kab and at Thebes.

The influence of local customs affected the Egyptian colonists in other ways than in their art. Prince Hepzefa, although he had provided an elaborate tomb for himself at home in Assiut, was unable to return there, dying at his post in Kerma in the reign of Amenemhat II. His burial, although badly disturbed, is probably to be reconstructed like that of the other great men at Kerma. The fu-neral must have been a peculiarly barbaric one. The body was laid out on a blue-glazed quartzite bed, of which fragments were found, although other burials at Kerma were on wooden beds like the reconstructed one in Fig. 63. This was placed in the central room of a complex of brick chambers which contained vari-ous articles of tomb equipment. Around the chief man lay the ladies of his harîm, and in an outer corridor were attendants and members of his household. The conditions under which the bodies of these people were found made it quite clear that they had been buried alive to accompany their master into the other world. They must have lain themselves down here for sacrificial burial on the day of the funeral, perhaps slightly drugged by the wine of the funeral feast, and allowed themselves to be covered with earth as the chambers were filled and a great tu-mulus heaped up over the burial.

Satî burial, as this kind of sacrificial death is called, was of course not prac-ticed in Egypt, although there is a hint that something of the sort may have been known in very early times. Here we find the strong influence of an African cus-tom which should have been abhorrent to a civilized Egyptian. Perhaps it was through the Nubian women in the harîm that a custom thoroughly prevalent in the Kerma district came to be adopted by the prince's household. That the Egyptians had a horror of foreign burial without a wooden coffin and the proper rites of purification is indicated over and over again in Egyptian literature. For instance, an Old Kingdom noble at Aswan made a dangerous expedition into Wawat (Nubia) to recover the body of his father who had been killed in battle there. Sinuhe, in a famous Middle Kingdom tale, begs to be allowed to return to Egypt from Palestine, so that he may not die there and be buried in the sand wrapped in a skin. However, there is no doubt that he would have been so buried had he died before Sesostris I gave him permission to return, and such must have been the case with Hepzefa, who received the bed-burial and accompanying rites in the Sudan. The latter took the precaution of contracting with funerary priests to carry out the proper ceremonies in his tomb at Assiut.

Amenemhat I probably succumbed to a second palace intrigue more successful than that which had troubled an earlier year of his reign. Certainly he died suddenly while his son was on an expedition against the Libyans of the western desert. The unexplained fear and flight to Palestine of Sinuhe, who was accompanying the prince, suggests that he knew more about the intrigue at the capital than was safe for him. Amenemhat I was buried in his pyramid at Lisht, and there his son, Sesostris I, also built a pyramid with a temple decorated with magnificent reliefs and a famous series of white limestone statues. Amenemhat II built his pyramid at Dahshur near Memphis, while Sesostris II constructed his at Lahun at the mouth of the Fayum. Sesostris III and Amenemhat III returned to Dahshur to build their tombs, but Amenemhat built a second pyramid at Hawara in the Fayum, where he was probably buried. Like his predecessors, Amenemhat III devoted particular attention to the development of the Fayum, an oasis with a large lake fed by a channel from the Nile which passes through a narrow break in the desert hills bordering the valley about fifty miles south of Cairo. By damming this channel the flow of water into the lake at high Nile was controlled, and the cutting of irrigation canals and the building of dykes reclaimed a large area of fertile land from the lake. In the time of Amenemhat III this area seems to have extended around the capital of the province, Shedet (Crocodilopolis), to the point on the south where Sesostris I had set up his peculiar obelisk at Begig, and on the northwest to Biahmu, where Amenemhat erected two colossal statues of himself on the edge of the lake. Beside his pyramid at Hawara, Amenemhat erected a huge structure which was famous in classical times under the name of the Labyrinth. Both Colossi and Labyrinth have almost entirely disappeared, but they were still standing to excite the wonder of Herodotus in the fifth century B.C.

In addition to their subjugation of the south, the Pharaohs of Dynasty XII resumed the mining operations in Sinai which had been allowed to lapse since the Old Kingdom. A more permanent establishment was organized at the mines and a temple dedicated to Hathor was built nearby. Amenemhat I seems to have skirmished with the Bedouins on the northeastern border and as a protection for the

Delta built a frontier fortress known as the ' Wall of the Prince.' Not until the reign of Sesostris III does there seem to have been a military expedition into Palestine, so that more or less peaceful relations must have been maintained. This is borne out by the friendly reception there of Sinuhe in the tale which gives an interesting picture of life among the Palestinian tribes. A sphinx with the name of one of the daughters of Amenemhat II was found at Qatna in Syria, while the statuette of another daughter, the wife of Sesostris II, was found at Ras Shamra (ancient Ugarit), as well as part of a sphinx with the name of Amenemhat III. Statues of important men who evidently represented the Egyptian government abroad have also been found. A fragmentary figure of the Vizier Sesostris-ankh was excavated at Ras Shamra, while at Megiddo there appeared the lower part of a statue of Djehuty-hetep, the Nomarch of Hermopolis, whose tomb at Bersheh has long been known. The parallel between this man and Hepzefa at Kerma is so close that it suggests greater political control in the north than was formerly admitted. There is much evidence for Egyptian influence at Byblos, the Syrian port which had been long visited by Egyptian shipping. Two of the native rulers buried there in the reigns of Amenemhat III and Amenemhat IV were supplied with equipment thoroughly Egyptian in design, although largely made by local workmen. The names and titles of these princes were written in Egyptian hieroglyphs which, from the peculiarities of writing, were probably not the work of an Egyptian scribe.

The pectorals and other jewels, as well as some of the weapons from Byblos, closely resemble the beautiful objects in Cairo and New York found in the princesses' tombs at Lahun and Dahshur. They are more coarsely made, however. The ornamented coffer and perfume vase, on the other hand, were probably sent as gifts to Byblos by the kings whose names are inscribed on them. Among the other objects from these tombs now in the Museum in Beirut, the peculiarly shaped battle-axes are in no way Egyptian, while the beautifully worked silver vases have close connections with the Aegean world. Silver vessels similarly decorated with spiral patterns and flutings, together with lapis lazuli evidently worked in Mesopotamia, were found buried in a chest under the temple of Tod near Thebes. This treasure, now in Cairo, perhaps represents tribute paid by the rulers of Byblos or some other important city in Syria. Middle Kingdom connections with Crete are certainly attested by the finding of sherds of the characteristic Kamares ware both at Kahun and Harageh, while a completely preserved vase of this type was placed in a Dynasty XII burial at Abydos. In Crete the statue of an Egyptian official of the Middle Kingdom was found at Knossos.

The reign of Amenemhat IV and that of Sebek-neferura have left little trace. The vigorous power of the dynasty seems to have come to an end with Amenemhat III. With the disappearance of Queen Sebek-neferura, who with the first king of Dynasty XIII, Amenemhat-Sebek-hotep, at least kept up the recording of the Nile levels at Semna, we reach a period of Egyptian history as dark as that between Dynasties VI and XI. This Second Intermediate Period falls into three partly overlapping divisions: Dynasties XIII-XIV, which carried on Middle King-dom traditions at Thebes and Memphis, the period of the Hyksos occupation (Dynasties XV-XVI), which began some eighty years before Dynasty XVII re-placed the kings of the early group at Thebes, and the time of the rebirth of Egyp-tian strength in Upper Egypt (Dynasty XVII). Over a stretch of nearly two hun-dred years we know less about events in Egypt than perhaps at any other period. It is possible to draw up a list of the names of kings, but their order is disputed and they have left few monuments. The first king of Dynasty XIII built a gate at Medamud in imitation of that of Sesostris III, while statues of some of his suc-cessors have been found at Karnak, in the Delta at Tanis, and in the Sudan at Argo and Kerma. King Khendjer built a pyramid near Dahshur, as did another of the later kings, while two other pyramids of this time are known at Mazghu-neh, not far away. The question of the origin of the Hyksos is not yet determined satisfactorily. Their descent into Egypt corresponds to upheavals in Western Asia which raise many problems not directly concerned with Egyptian history. That their capital was at Avaris in the eastern part of the Delta is certain. One of their kings, Khian, is known outside Egypt from an inscribed jar lid found in Crete and a lion purchased in Baghdad for the British Museum. Several other kings bearing the name of Apepi are known by scarcely more than their names. As in the wars between Thebes and Heracleopolis, what few records there are of this period are mostly concerned with the war of liberation fought by the kings of Dynasty XVII against the Asiatic oppressors. Ahmose finally succeeded in driving the invaders out of the Delta, capturing their capital Avaris and pursuing them into Palestine, where he laid siege to the stronghold of Sharuhen. One of his soldiers tells us that he also raided the land of Djahi (the Phoenician coast) after taking Sharuhen. The Hyksos power was therefore finally broken.

THE ARTS AND CRAFTS OF THE MIDDLE KINGDOM

THE GREAT ARCHITECTURAL PROJECTS of the Middle Kingdom have largely dis-appeared under the rebuilding of the Pharaohs of the New Kingdom. Except for the temple of Mentuhotep at Deir el Bahari described on p. 71, the only two well-preserved monuments are buildings of modest proportions. One of these is a little shrine of Sesostris I recently restored by Chevrier from blocks built into later structures at Karnak. It was a small kiosk surrounded by square columns set upon a high base, and served as a pavilion for the Heb Sed festival. It was decorated with very fine low reliefs. On the southern edge of the Fayum at Medi-net el Maadi the Italian excavators found a small temple bearing the names of Amenemhat III and IV. The shrine at the back is still standing nearly complete. Entered from the center of its long wall is a cross hall from which three chapels open at the back. The reliefs are rather heavy in style and not very well propor-tioned. The pyramid temples of Sesostris I and Amenemhat I at Lisht are the only funerary structures sufficiently excavated to study in detail. Although badly preserved, they resemble closely pyramid temples of the Old Kingdom.

That the Middle Kingdom rulers initiated that taste for grandiose scale in temple architecture so characteristic of the New Kingdom is evident from the impression which the Labyrinth at Hawara made upon classical travellers. It is more than hinted at by the great obelisk which is all that remains from the temple of Sesostris I at Heliopolis, or the huge architectural members of the Delta temples. Much of this material was usurped by later kings, and it is possible that two columns and a capital in this collection were originally from Middle Kingdom temples. The papyrus bundle-column (Fig. 44) and a Hathor capital (Fig. 46) were found in a great hall of the Dynasty XIX temple at Bubastis, but huge architraves discovered with them had been usurped by Ramesses II from Sesostris III. It is possible that these were all part of a columned hall built in Dynasty XII. The same sort of usurpation may have occurred in the case of a palm column which formed part of a portico in the temple at Heracleopolis (Ehnasiya) (Fig. 43). It bears the names of both Ramesses and Merenptah, but the temple was built over an earlier structure and contained architectural fragments inscribed with the name of Sesostris III. There is little either in the proportions or the treatment of details to distinguish this column from the Old Kingdom form as it is found in the temples of Sahura and Unas. The same type of column was used to support the portico of the tomb of Djehuty-hetep at Bersheh in Dynasty XII. The papyrus bundle-column also was used in Dynasty V, but the form is much heavier in our example, and the colossal size would not have been found at an earlier period. The Hathor column was never very common in Egyptian architecture and is otherwise unknown until Dynasty XVIII. While it is not impossible that these three pieces were actually made for the Dynasty XIX temples in which they were found, the suggestion that they were usurped elements from structures of Dynasty XII can be accepted without serious objection.

The polygonal column with plain or channelled faces is common in the Middle Kingdom, both in the rock-cut tombs, as in the famous examples at Beni Hasan, and in the temples such as that of Mentuhotep at Deir el Bahari. No. 07.535 is a fragment from one of these Deir el Bahari columns with the king's name in sunk relief filled with blue paint. The form is found as early as Dynasty III at the Step Pyramid, where bundles of reeds are imitated, and at least one example of Dynasty IV is known at Giza. Perhaps the most effective use of this column, which has often been called 'Proto-Doric' from its somewhat superficial resemblance to the Greek order, is in the terraces of Hatshepsut's Dynasty XVIII temple at Deir el Bahari. Still another column derived from plant forms is that imitating lotus flowers and buds tied together in a fashion resembling the papyrus bundle-column. This attractive support is found in the Old Kingdom in the tomb of Ptah-shepses at Abusir and in a more slender version at Beni Hasan in the Middle Kingdom. It remained for Dynasty XVIII to evolve the stone campaniform papyrus column, although representations of it constructed in light materials to support shrines and small buildings are known as early as Dynasty III.

43. *Right:* Palm column

44. *Left:* Papyrus column

45. Pottery 'Soul House'

46. Hathor capital

The rock-cut tombs of the nobles have preserved some of the best examples of the architecture of Dynasty XII. The façades of the Beni Hasan tombs with their polygonal columns supporting an architrave imitating wooden timbering are familiar to every traveller in Egypt. Similar façades appear in the tombs at Rifeh. These entrances open upon a hall with columns cut from the rock as the room was excavated. At the back of the hall is a shrine intended for a statue. Similar tombs are found at Aswan and Meir, but these lack the portico on the façade. The tomb of Hepzefa at Assiut elaborates the ground plan with an entrance hall and larger shrine, while the excavation is on a truly enormous scale. At Thebes the bad quality of the rock discouraged the use of wide columned halls, which were replaced by a long narrow corridor leading to an offering chamber at the back. In the tombs of Dynasty XI there was often a portico supported by heavy piers. The most original treatment is found in the tombs of Qau el Kebir which rise in terraces with columned porticoes or halls connected by staircases and ending in a large rock-cut offering room on the upper level. Each level is fronted by a pylon-like wall and the lowest is entered by a long covered way from the valley edge, as in Old Kingdom funerary temples. These tombs seem to form a link between the temple of Mentuhotep and the terraced temple of Hatshepsut at Deir el Bahari. Certain wooden models and the pottery ' soul houses,' like Nos. 07.550, 551 in this collection (Fig. 45), suggest that the Qau el Kebir tombs may also reflect a fairly common house type with a staircase leading from a court with a columned portico to an upper story with a loggia opening on the court. All these tombs of Dynasty XII are elaborately decorated either with painted scenes or carvings in fine relief. The ceilings, which are usually cut in the form of a shallow barrel vault, are enlivened with gay patterns imitating mat-work or with designs made up of scrolls, stars, palmettes, or spirals.

The style of the Middle Kingdom wall decorations, both in painting and reliefs, is a blending of Old Kingdom forms with newer elements. A vigorous, rather harsh quality, combined with elongated, more angular proportions, seems to have been an Upper Egyptian development of the First Intermediate Period (Figs. 47, 48). The style, as we have said before, is by no means as uniform as it was in the Old Kingdom. Marked local peculiarities make themselves felt, while in those districts where Memphite influence remained strong there is a closer resemblance to Old Kingdom work. This is evident in the reliefs at Meir as well as in many of the blocks from the temple of Sesostris I at Lisht. Everywhere the subject matter of the Old Kingdom scenes remained in use and frequently the arrangement of the scenes resembled the older models. The repertoire of scenes was considerably enlarged and there was a tendency to amplify the backgrounds with representations of buildings, trees, and accessories. Thus the action of a group of figures acquires a more definite setting. The draughtsmanship and elaborate indication of details are meticulous, even when the forms delineated are somewhat harsh and awkward. The high relief of early Dynasty XI with its rather cramped forms and intricate detail gave place to a broader treatment as in

47. Burial stela from Gebelein. First Intermediate Period

the modelling of the royal head from the temple of Mentuhotep II (Fig. 42). In the reign of Se-ankh-kara the cutting of the reliefs was lower and was further refined by delicate surface modelling which was graded smoothly into the background. Such delicate low reliefs continued into Dynasty XII in the tombs at Qau el Kebir and the royal monuments of Sesostris I. But the wall decorations of that king at Lisht vary considerably. A high, bold type of carving was frequently employed, as in the sculptured panels of the enclosing wall of the pyramid. The hawk (No. 37.590) surmounted the king's Horus name in one of the panels of this wall. The bold carving is again well-illustrated by the detail of a bird from the reliefs of the Pyramid Temple of Sesostris I at Lisht (Fig. 49). The wall reliefs of the kings who followed Sesostris I have not been recovered in such great quantity. Nevertheless, enough remains to make it clear that a high average of excellence was maintained throughout the dynasty.

The painting of the Middle Kingdom, applied as it was to the walls of rock-cut tombs, has remained for the most part in Egypt. In the outer coffin of Prince Djehuty-nekht from Bersheh we have, however, a superlative example of Dynasty XII painting. While the Bersheh coffins are in general better painted than those from any other site, they do not ordinarily attain such fine quality as in

48. Details of painted wooden coffin. First Intermediate Period

this example (Fig. 51). In fact the inner coffin of this man and the outer and inner coffins of his wife present the more ordinary workmanship which it is natural to expect from the shop of a maker of funerary equipment. A painter of unusual ability lavished special care on the inner faces of Djehuty-nekht's great cedar sarcophagus. Against the soft brown tones of the wood which forms the background, figures and hieroglyphs have been minutely executed in brilliant color that has the enamel-like quality of miniature painting (Fig. 52). On one wall the prince is shown seated beside an elaborate false-door receiving the offering presented by an attendant (Fig. 50). Birds, meat-pieces, cakes, fruits, vegetables, and flowers are heaped up around the table and accompanied by a list of offerings each item of which is set in a separate compartment. On the opposite wall, beneath an inscription in ornamental hieroglyphs, is a frieze of garments, necklaces, tools, and weapons. These are interspersed with magical staves, a lion-headed bed, a bull's hide shield and quiver, as well as brilliantly colored fan and mirror cases. A large part of the surface is covered with magical texts in vertical columns of small incised hieroglyphs. These texts contain a large part of the Pyramid Texts of the Old Kingdom which had been appropriated by the Nomarchs of the Intermediate Period. They retain much of the old phraseology which was intended for the king's use and is scarcely suitable for a private person. New elements were added, however, and one of these, ' The Book of the Two Ways,' appears on the inner coffin of Djehuty-nekht. It was a kind of map, or chart, intended to guide the dead man through the perilous places of the Underworld.

The play of influences is not so easy to analyze in the Middle Kingdom sculpture in the round. The breakdown of the all-pervading Memphite school had a decisive effect upon the statues. While the harsh realism of the Theban school produced some of the most extraordinary portraits ever carved in Egypt, the revived Old Kingdom style seems to lack vitality. The freshness so apparent in the draughtsmanship at Meir and Lisht is less evident in the plastic form. The statues following along the old lines achieved technical dexterity but they have lost something of the strength and vigor which made the royal sculpture of the Old Kingdom so impressive. Such figures as the seated limestone statues of Sesostris I from Lisht in the Cairo Museum leave an impression of over-smoothness and

49. Relief from temple of Sesostris I at Lisht

50. Painted panel of Bersheh coffin

conventionality. Moreover, the private sculpture, in freeing itself from the bounds of the older conventional proportions, gained a new variety of form, but it lost some of the sureness of balance and design which gave such a pleasing appearance to the average private statue of Dynasty V. The indiscriminate use of inscriptions over sculptured surfaces, which was to become so prevalent in the New Kingdom, begins in these statues. Voluminous wigs, cloaks, and long robes give these figures a heaviness that had been avoided in Memphite art. Good examples which illustrate this are the excellently worked seated figures of two Egyptian officials from Kerma (Nos. 14.721, 723). The portly figures of both men are wrapped in long fringed robes, while they wear full wigs of the curious Middle Kingdom type.

Such a statue as that of Wepwawet-em-hat from Assiut (Fig. 53) gives us a very good idea of the kind of sculpture that emerged at the end of the First Intermediate Period. The exact date is uncertain. It probably belongs to Dynasty X, toward the end of the period of Heracleopolitan rule. In workmanship it corresponds to the renewal of good painting in the chapel of Tef-ib, or the well-cut warriors in sunk relief on the walls of Khety's tomb. The craftsmen of Assiut seem to have been a little ahead of their contemporaries, except those at Thebes. Our statue has the stark quality that we have found in the Theban art of Dynasty XI. Rude strength is the chief impression produced by it, but the representation of the human body here is a long step beyond the meagre stick-like forms of the sculptors of Dynasties VIII and IX. The model servant figures found with this statue were surprisingly well carved. Two of them are also in this collection: a group of men slaughtering an ox (No. 04.1781) and a black and white spotted bull (No. 04.1778).

The next step in advance is well-illustrated by the sandstone head of Mentuhotep wearing the white crown from one of the statues of this king in the form of Osiris (No. 07.536). The causeway of Mentuhotep's temple at Deir el Bahari was lined with such standing and seated figures. Similar Osiride statues were often placed against the square pillars of a temple court, while at Lisht white limestone figures of Sesostris I in this form stood at intervals along the inner walls of the causeway corridor.

We have in this collection no royal work of Dynasty XII under Memphite influence. Perhaps a reflection of this style is to be sought, however, in the statue of the Lady Sennuwy, one of the most appealing works of the period. This seated figure of the wife of Hepzefa, the Egyptian governor of Kerma, was found buried in his funeral mound (Fig. 54). It strikes a peculiarly civilized note in the midst of that barbaric burial. Probably this statue, as well as that of the lady's husband which was recovered in a fragmentary condition, was made by a sculptor whom Hepzefa had brought with other craftsmen of his household from Assiut. The beautifully proportioned figure of the woman, as well as the delicate beauty of the face and the smooth finish given to the gray granite, make one think of the Lisht statues of Sesostris I, in whose reign the figure was probably made.

51. Detail of the Bersheh coffin

Opposite: 52. Detail of the Bersheh coffin

Opposite: 53. Wooden statue of Wepwawet-em-hat from Assiut

54. Head of granite seated statue of the lady Sennuwy

55. Statuette of Sesostris III from Sinai

The brutal strain of realism which ran through most of the portrait heads in hard stone of early Dynasty XII culminated in the magnificent heads of Sesostris III, unparalleled for grim strength, and in the somewhat softer features of Amenemhat III. The characteristic features of Sesostris III appear on a small scale in the little statuette of that king found in the Hathor Temple at Sinai (Fig. 55). In the green stone head from Kerma (Fig. 56), unfortunately preserved only in a fragment, we possess one of the most sensitive of the studies of Amenemhat III. As in most statues of these two reigns, the sculptor seized upon the salient features of the king and exaggerated them. Deeply etched lines at the corners of the mouth and pouches beneath the eyes well suggest a weary and disillusioned nature. It is a more sensitive face than that of Amenemhat's hard and relentless predecessor, Sesostris III, who is perhaps represented in the small bust of dark stone (No. 13.3968). Reflected in the faces of these men is the same bitter note that pervades the literature of the Middle Kingdom. Similar in treatment to the green head is the face carved in brown quartzite (No. 28.1). Since it bears no royal insignia it may represent Amenemhat III while still crown prince. The

56. Head of Amenemhat III from Kerma

57. Head of wooden statue of a king from Kerma

wooden statue of an unknown king from Kerma (Fig. 57) closes our series of
royal portraits. It dates from Dynasty XIII at a time approaching the Hyksos
Period and begins to suggest the work of the New Kingdom. Although the ears
are still large and prominent as in Middle Kingdom heads, the face has assumed
a more conventional aspect, marred somewhat by the loss of the inlaid eyes. The
slenderness of the tall figure and the pronounced narrowness of the waist herald
the lighter, more graceful proportions of Dynasty XVIII.

Toward the end of the Old Kingdom the custom of placing figures of servants
in the burial chamber had developed into the making of elaborate models which
were intended to serve the same purpose as the scenes from life painted on the
walls of the chapel. These continued into the Middle Kingdom, and the great cedar coffins of Djehuty-nekht and his wife at Bersheh were accompanied by many
models, most of them showing different kinds of river boats with their crews.
Perhaps the most interesting of these is a large vessel with a cabin, at the entrance to which was placed a little table, tipped-up on end, and the noble's travelling trunk painted to imitate ox hide (No. 21.406). A small cooking galley contained a man fanning a charcoal fire (No. 21.407). There were also models of men
plowing (No. 21.408) and one showing the making of bricks (No. 21.411). While
most of these are very crudely made, one procession is unusually well carved. It
shows a portly, light-skinned overseer carrying a mirror in a gaily painted case,
while behind him follow three women laden with live ducks and boxes of provisions (Fig. 58). The slender, well-modelled figures and the delicacy of the carved
and painted detail are in strong contrast to the roughness of the other models.
The group stands out as sharply from these servant figures as does the outer coffin of its owner, Djehuty-nekht, from most painted coffins of the time. The same
superlative craftsmanship appears in both and the wooden procession does not
suffer by comparison with the paintings which it so closely resembles in style.

A similar delicacy is to be found in another wood carving from this tomb. It is
a model censer with a tiny box to contain the pellets of incense attached to the
handle, which ends in a human hand grasping the spoon-shaped receptacle (No.
20.1124) (Fig. 60). Two exquisitely worked wooden figures of naked women were
part of a group of delightful small objects from a neighboring burial at Bersheh
(Fig. 60). With them was found a tiny wooden head of a woman with a remarkable headdress. The neck was probably attached to a wand or handle, but what
the complete object can have been is uncertain (Fig. 60). A ram-headed figure of
the god Khnum is carved from ivory, but unfortunately is not complete (No. 21.-
928). A tiny hedgehog and hippopotamus made of dark blue faience also formed
part of this pleasing group (Nos. 20.1119, 1118).

The stone vessels of the Middle Kingdom are generally small jars or pots intended for ointments and cosmetics, but the tall, slender shoulder jar from Kerma is an unusually large and splendid specimen (Fig. 59). It must have been
valued by its owner both for the beautiful material and graceful shape. Although
the pottery of the period from Egypt consists of not very attractive cooking and

58. Model procession from Bersheh

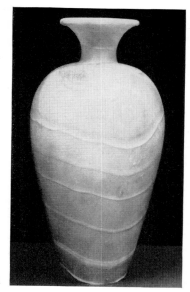

59. Alabaster vase from Kerma

60. Small carvings in wood from Bersheh

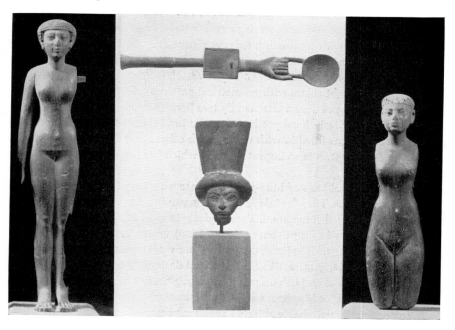

61. Pottery and faience from Kerma

storage vessels, the shining, polished red and black ware from Kerma attracts immediate attention. The texture and thinness of the ware are as remarkable as the shapes, which are sometimes quite bizarre. Most common are the tall beaker-like forms, but those with undulating sides are quite frequent, and the potter was fond of making vessels with long, very slender spouts (Fig. 61). A few small pots with conical lids, and occasionally a larger vessel, were made of a grayish ware and painted in bright colors with geometrical patterns (Nos. 20.1691-1693). One vase has a painting of a man attacked by two lions (No. 20.1694). These seem to have been a peculiarly local product, but the jug (No. 20.1700) of black ware with incised designs filled in with white is like others found at a number of different sites in Egypt. It is an imported fabric which has been associated with the Hyksos invaders.

The making of objects of blue-glazed faience was one of the most developed of the Kerma crafts. Tiles for inlaying in walls were common, although no single example is preserved complete. Elaborate designs must have been attempted, to judge from the head of a prisoner (No. 20.1305) whose bound arms are on another piece, or the striding lions, of which there were a number of fragmentary examples. Particularly attractive are the varied designs of flying birds combined with plants, animals, and fish on many bowl fragments (Fig. 61). From Egypt itself comes the faience hippopotamus (Fig. 62).

Many ordinarily perishable objects have been preserved in the dry sand of Up-

62. Faience hippopotamus

per Egypt and the Sudan to give us a clear idea of the garments, weapons, and household furnishings of the period. From Sheikh Farag, a cemetery which was probably used by the same community that buried its dead at Naga-ed-Dêr, comes a wig made of tiny braids of false hair (No. 13.4356). At Kerma were found fans made of ostrich feathers (No. 13.4198) and a fragment of a rug with a long nap laid on coarse linen canvas backing (No. 20.1492). String nets for carrying water pots were also found at Kerma and woven pieces of giraffe hair which may be parts of caps.

A variety of animal shapes were cut out of mica for decorating leather caps, while similar animals were carved from ivory to be inlaid into the footboards of beds (Figs. 63-64). The well-preserved wooden hoe (No. 21.833) was found at Bersheh, while a number of baskets that look as though they had been freshly woven come from Sheikh Farag. At the latter place were recovered good examples of the weapons of the period, such as the copper-tipped spear and arrows, or the wooden bow and the battle-axe with its copper blade. More unusual are the daggers from Kerma with elaborate pommels of ivory and copper studded with heavy rivet-heads (Nos. 13.4016, 20.1566). A profusion of metal knives, razors, tweezers, axe-heads, and harpoon-points were found at Kerma. Particularly attractive is the knife with a duck's head curved around at the tip (No. 20.-1799). Wooden throwing sticks like those represented in the scenes of hunting birds in the marshes were found at Kerma and Naga-ed-Dêr. Characteristic of

63. Reproduction of a bed from Kerma

the Middle Kingdom are the ivory wands decorated with mythical animals (No. 03.1703), or the ivory and copper emblems in the form of a fly (No. 20.1776) which were perhaps distributed as a military decoration. Ivory spoons were also elaborately carved like the little piece with the goose's head from Sheikh Farag (No. 13.3727).

In addition to the small vessels of hard stone, the tweezers, and sticks for dipping out eye-paint, the most commonly found toilet articles are the mirrors. Two of these from Kerma are the product of considerable skill (Nos. 20.1790, 1792). The handles are cast in a braided design, while one has gold rivets and silver sheathing on the handle. These mirrors, as well as the silver uraeus (Fig. 66), the curiously studded silver amulet, the electrum shells, and gold cowrie necklace (Fig. 65) from various sites excavated by our Expedition remind us that the jewelers' art had reached a level in the Middle Kingdom never excelled at any other time in Egypt. Typical of the period are the magnificent necklaces of amethyst and carnelian beads, sometimes with the stones separated by gold spacers. Broad collars of faience, occasionally with hawk-headed end pieces, continued to be made following the form of the Old Kingdom necklace. Although less rich in material, these ornaments made for the nobles of Dynasty XII show the same fine craftsmanship that appears in the famous Cairo Museum jewelry of the princesses from Dahshur and Lahun, which was imitated even in far off Syria for the rulers of Byblos.

64. Ivory inlays from Kerma

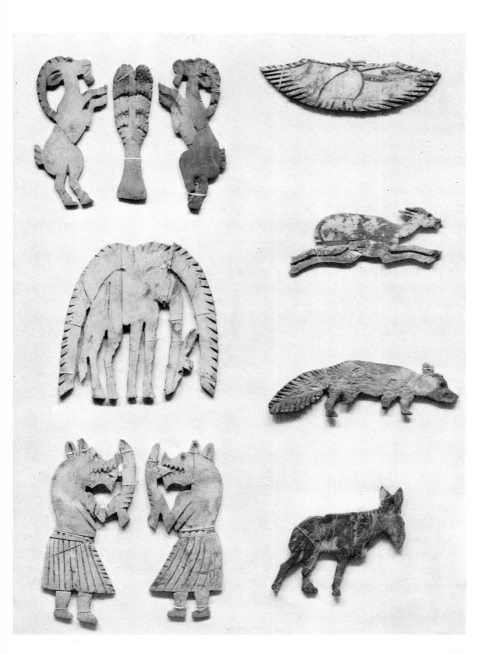

65. Necklaces from Uronarti and Kerma, electrum shell from Sheikh Farag

66. Silver uraeus from Naga-ed-Dêr

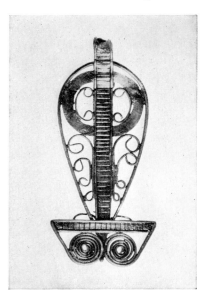

Chapter IV

The New Kingdom

THE HISTORICAL BACKGROUND: DYNASTY XVIII

AHMOSE, by pursuing the Hyksos into Palestine, not only freed Egypt from Asiatic oppression but committed his successors to a foreign policy entirely different from that pursued in the past. The Hyksos had taught Egypt the bitter lesson that strong powers were rising in Western Asia, which could no longer be controlled by a raiding party into Palestine or the possession of trading stations on the coast like Byblos. Nothing short of the conquest and continued domination of the little kingdoms to the northeast could ensure the safety of Egypt's borders. Gradually, with the stimulation of further military success in the reign of Tuthmosis I, there came the new conception of Egypt as a world power, which was realized by the campaigns of Tuthmosis III. This great ruler created an empire which stretched from the Euphrates in the northeast to Napata in the south.

Although Egypt had not been without foreign contacts in the past, Dynasty XVIII brought a closer relationship with the lands beyond the narrow Nile Valley. Events abroad now came to have a practical meaning to the citizen of Thebes or Memphis. Ordinary men like Ahmose, son of Abana, and Ahmose Pen-nekhbet, from the town of El Kab far up the Nile, returned home from the banks of the Euphrates to tell their neighbors of wars in foreign lands. Embassies from Crete, Assyria, and Babylon arrived in the capital bearing strange gifts. New tongues were heard in the streets of the large Egyptian towns, spoken by these foreign envoys and by the slaves brought back by conquering armies. With the fully developed Empire we find Tuthmosis IV marrying a daughter of the King of Mitanni. For two generations his successors received as wives ladies of this family, as well as Babylonian princesses, who travelled to Egypt in great pomp with large retinues. Amenhotep III even negotiated with the King of Arzawa on the Asia Minor coast for his daughter in marriage. The balance of power among the Hittites, Mitanni, and the Kassite Dynasty of Babylon had to be maintained by diplomacy or by force of arms. Amenhotep III and Akhenaten corresponded and exchanged presents with these great powers as well as with the growing Kingdom of Assyria and with the King of Cyprus. These far off countries became as important to Egyptian policy as the squabbling little kingdoms nearer at hand in Palestine and Syria, or the maintenance of peace in Ethiopia.

In the diplomatic correspondence known as the Tell el Amarna letters we can see this whole fabric crumbling, weakened by Amenhotep III's system of bribing allegiance by doles of gold and by the increasing neglect of his son, the religious fanatic Akhenaten. But Egypt's prestige in Asia was to be regained in Dynasty XIX, and never again was she able to return to the safe isolation of the past. We must expect, therefore, a more complex civilization in the New Kingdom than that which existed in previous periods. The old simplicity of life was gone forever, lost in the variety of new currents and the luxury provided by foreign booty. Dynasty XVIII was the most brilliant of all the epochs in Egyptian history, a time when a people enormously invigorated by its successful struggle for freedom was eagerly absorbing a wealth of new influences.

Amenhotep I was a son of Ahmose by his queen Ahmes-Nofretari, and mother and son came to be revered in later times not only as founders of the dynasty but as the tutelary deities of the Theban Necropolis. The women of this family seem to have maintained a peculiarly important position, although throughout Egyptian history the descent of the blood royal on the woman's side had always been a factor determining the legitimacy of an aspirant to the throne. In this case we have a succession of able women who did much to guide the fortunes of the dynasty and who go far toward explaining the unusual phenomenon of Hatshepsut, who actually became ruler of the country with all the powers of a king. First there was Teti-sheri, the wife of Taa-aa, who is known to us from her charming statuettes. She was the first of a series of queen-mothers who seem to have dealt with domestic affairs while their sons were engaged in military campaigns. Her children were Ah-hotep and Sekenenra. When Sekenenra was killed, either in battle with the Hyksos or in a palace conspiracy, his wife, Ah-hotep, served in turn as regent for Kamose. Kamose after a brief reign was succeeded by his brother, Ahmose, whose wife was Queen Ahmes-Nofretari. This lady acted as regent for her son, Amenhotep I, who was married to Ah-hotep II. The old queen Ah-hotep may have lived on into this reign.

Palestine and Syria apparently remained quiet during the reign of Amenhotep I. His father's conquests had evidently been sufficient for this, but it was necessary to lead an important expedition into Ethiopia. This is reported by the two El Kab warriors who participated in most of the military campaigns of the early part of Dynasty XVIII. The account of the long career of the court official Inene begins with this reign and records the death of the king. His successor, Tuthmosis I, was the son of a minor queen, and legitimized his position by marrying Ahmes, the daughter of Queen Ah-hotep II. Thus yet another in the long line of royal ladies played her part in dynastic affairs. The king's coronation proclamation is addressed to the first Viceroy of Nubia of whom we have knowledge, which means that a new step had been taken in the administration of the country to the south of Egypt. That Nubia was still not completely controlled is shown by the expedition which the king was forced to make in his second year when he seems to have conquered the country as far south as the Fourth Cataract. He returned with a captive chieftain hanging from the prow of his ship. Next Tuthmo-sis I undertook a Syrian campaign which carried him into Nahrin where he set up a boundary stela on the banks of the Euphrates.

Tuthmosis II, like his father, was the son of a lesser queen, but he strength-ened his claim to the throne by marrying Hatshepsut, the daughter of the chief queen Ahmes. Suffering from ill health, he evidently realized only too well the domineering qualities of his wife, for he took pains to establish as his successor the young son born to him by the lady Isit. Tuthmosis III later tells us that, while serving as a youthful priest in a ceremony at Karnak at which his father was officiating, the image of Amon singled him out and, by an oracle, chose him as king. Nevertheless, the early death of Tuthmosis II left the young prince un-der the regency of Hatshepsut. The latter at first respected the conventional forms of the regency. Tuthmosis III was married to her daughter Neferura, who seems to have played little part in the events that followed and probably died young. Hatshepsut in this phase of her career built a tomb in which she calls her-self simply ' King's Wife.'

Hatshepsut was supported by a group of able and powerful men which in-cluded her favorite Senmut, the architect of Deir el Bahari, his brother Senmen, Nehery, the leader of the Punt expedition, and Hapu-seneb under whom were cleverly combined the offices both of Vizier and High Priest of Amon. Hatshep-sut soon felt powerful enough, with this able support, to declare herself supreme ruler of the country, not as queen regent, but as king. In the reliefs of the funer-ary temple at Deir el Bahari, which she commenced at this time, is built up an elaborate fiction to support her rule as king. Not only is she represented in male dress and with the royal beard, but she is shown crowned by her father Tuth-mosis I. As in the case of other rulers, the legitimacy of whose claims was uncer-tain, Hatshepsut represents herself as the daughter of the state god Amon, who came to her mother Ahmes in the guise of that lady's husband, Tuthmosis I. Tuthmosis III was relegated to the background, and there is no better evidence of the ability of Hatshepsut than that this energetic and determined youth, who later became one of the most powerful kings of Egypt, was unable to exhibit his latent powers until after Hatshepsut's death. It is hardly surprising that he hated this woman and her coterie of advisers, and that he ruthlessly blotted out every sign that they had ever existed.

As part of her plan of associating herself with her father, Hatshepsut joined the cult of Tuthmosis I to her own in her funerary temple. But she went even further, deciding to transfer the body of Tuthmosis I to a new tomb which she was having prepared for herself as king of Egypt. Her coffin, which had just been completed, was re-cut to display the name and titles of her father, while an even finer sarcophagus was commenced for the queen. This rather shoddy treatment of Tuthmosis I, combined with the grandiloquent statement of the honors she was paying her father, must have particularly infuriated Tuthmosis III. When he finally came to power, he seems to have had a new quartzite coffin made for his

105

grandfather, and removed him from the hated association with Hatshepsut back to his original tomb, the one that Inene had long ago prepared, ' no one seeing, no one hearing.' It is very doubtful that Hatshepsut received a decent burial from her nephew, in spite of the two tombs and three granite coffins which she had successively ordered as her power increased.

The twenty-one peaceful years of Hatshepsut's reign were prosperous ones for Egypt. She concentrated her attention upon the inner administration of the country and upon great building enterprises. She undertook the restoration of monuments ravaged by the Hyksos, which her predecessors, engaged in foreign wars, had found no time to repair. Her one great foreign enterprise was of a commercial nature, the ambitious trading expedition to Punt so magnificently recorded in the reliefs of the Deir el Bahari temple. It is probable that the lack of strong measures taken in Syria necessitated the campaigns of Tuthmosis III, but the queen left behind her a well organized and wealthy country which enabled the new king to devote his attention to foreign conquest. It is evident that the two achievements of which Hatshepsut was most proud were the Punt expedition and the raising of the two great obelisks at Karnak. Both were intended to celebrate her devotion to her father Amon. It was primarily to bring back incense for the god that Hatshepsut sent her fleet down the Red Sea to the Somali Coast. With an unusual wealth of detail, the Deir el Bahari reliefs represent the reception of the leader of the expedition, Nehery, by the chief of Punt and his enormously fat wife. We can see the mat huts of his village set on piles and surrounded by groves of palm and incense trees. The artists have represented the strange birds and animals, even the fish, of this far off land with the same interest which prompted Tuthmosis III to have the plants and animals of Syria recorded on the walls of a room in the temple of Karnak. Hatshepsut's ships are shown being loaded with the incense, and even the incense-bearing trees themselves, with gold, panther skins, and ebony logs, as well as rare animals. After a successful return to Thebes, the methodical recording of all this temple wealth by the scribes is shown.

The Deir el Bahari reliefs also show the transport of the queen's obelisks, a work which was undertaken by Senmut. These were set up in a hall built by her father at Karnak which had been partially demolished for the purpose. One is broken and the upper part lies on the debris nearby, but the other obelisk still stands in its original position, the tallest one left in Egypt. When Tuthmosis III undertook his considerable building operations at Karnak, he reconstructed this hall of his grandfather, and walled up the obelisks so that visitors passing down the central axis of the temple would not notice that they were there and could not read the inscriptions eulogizing Hatshepsut's great works.

At last, twenty-one years after the death of his father, Tuthmosis III came into his own rights. A mature man who had long chafed under the oppression of his hated aunt, he turned as soon as she was dead to the military projects for which he was so admirably gifted. The immediate occasion for prompt action was the revolt of the Prince of Kadesh who, encouraged by the Kingdom of Mitanni, had organized a coalition of city states from Sharuhen in the south to the Euphrates in the north. After occupying Gaza in the year 23, Tuthmosis proceeded against Megiddo where the forces of the coalition had advanced to meet him. Swiftly moving his troops through a little-used and narrow pass, the king outflanked the combined armies of his enemies and defeated them in a pitched battle. He then laid siege to the fortress of Megiddo, in which the chieftains had taken refuge with the remainder of their armies. With the surrender of Megiddo all the country as far as the southern Lebanon came under the control of Egypt. Tuthmosis soon showed, however, that he had ambitions far beyond what had been accomplished so far.

The campaigns of the years 24 to 28 are meagrely recorded, although in the first of these years envoys were sent from Assyria with presents, and a record of the plants and animals of Syria was carved upon the walls of a room at Karnak. In his fifth campaign, Tuthmosis made secure the coast and harbors of Djahi (Phoenicia) as a foundation for his plan to attack Kadesh, and in his sixth campaign he transported his troops by sea to Djahi and captured Kadesh. The next year was spent in equipping the Phoenician harbors for an expedition to Nahrin, the country of the Mitannians, which was undertaken in the eighth campaign of the year 33. Carchemish was captured and a defeat inflicted on the king of Mitanni. Having crossed the Euphrates, Tuthmosis set up a boundary stela beside that of his grandfather, Tuthmosis I. The far-reaching repercussions of his success were clearly marked by the arrival of envoys of the kings of Babylon and the Hittites. A revolt of the kingdom of Mitanni called Tuthmosis III back into Nahrin in the year 35, while further punitive expeditions had to be made into the southern Lebanon and into Palestine in the years 38 and 39. During this time gifts were received from the Prince of Cyprus and from Assyria. A much more serious rebellion was the cause of his last campaign in the year 42. Again its central focus was Kadesh, assisted by Nahrin and Tunip. Both Kadesh and Tunip were completely crushed this time and the strength of Mitanni was so shattered that friendly relations with Nahrin were maintained throughout the following reigns. In all, Tuthmosis had undertaken seventeen campaigns into the north and had established a fear of Egyptian arms which would long command respect in Syria and Northern Mesopotamia. Egypt was firmly established as a world power with a far-reaching empire.

From no other reign do we have such complete records as those supplied by the Annals which Tuthmosis caused to be engraved in the great temple of Amon at Karnak. Unfortunately they have been very much condensed from the leather rolls on which a day by day account was taken down by an eyewitness of the action. Therefore they do not all have the factual detail of the description of the battle and siege of Megiddo. It is probable that we have in Zanene the author of some of the later field reports who tells us in his tomb that he accompanied the king and recorded his victories in writing. The biography of the general Amenemhab, in his Theban tomb, adds details omitted in the official records, such as the interesting account of the elephant hunt at Niy, which is also referred to by the king in our stela from Gebel Barkal. Intef the Herald tells us that it was his duty to precede the king abroad in order to prepare the Syrian palaces for his reception and residence. Other events came to be woven into popular tales like that of the surprise of Joppa by General Djehuty, who concealed his men in sacks and thus introduced them into the beleaguered city, much as in the tale of Ali Baba and the Forty Thieves.

Amenhotep II seems to have inherited many of his father's energetic qualities. A stela recently found near the Sphinx at Giza tells us that it was set up when the prince became king, in order to commemorate the joy which he had felt in contemplating the monuments of Cheops and Chephren when, as a youth, he drove out in his chariot from Memphis. It boasts of the king's accomplishments as an oarsman, bowman, and horseman, and tells us that as a boy his father recognized his skill and gave him the run of his stables. Elsewhere is recorded Amenhotep's personal prowess in the Asiatic campaigns which he undertook early in his reign. Amenhotep II claims to have overwhelmed Nahrin (Mitanni) but he apparently did not advance much farther north of Ugarit than Alalakh in the Antioch Plain. He brought back seven princes from the region of Takhsy near Kadesh. Of these he made a terrible example, hanging six from the walls of Thebes and the seventh at Napata in Kush. The king later made a derisive reference to Alalakh and Takhsy in a letter written on the feast of his accession to his Viceroy of Nubia, Weser-satet, who recorded it on our stela from the Semna cataract fortress (No. 25.632).

Tuthmosis IV, who succeeded his father, also erected a stela at Giza. On it he recounts how, on a hunting expedition, he fell asleep in the shadow of the Sphinx during the heat of the day. The Sun God appeared to him in a dream, telling him that he would ascend the throne of Egypt and asking him to clear away the sand which had accumulated around his image. When he became king, Tuthmosis carried out the required restorations and set up as a memorial of his pious response to this prophecy the magnificent stela which still stands between the paws of the Sphinx. There is an obvious resemblance between this inscription and that on the stela of Amenhotep II in the brick temple nearby. It is easy to imagine that an awe-inspiring monument like the Sphinx, originally made as an image of King Chephren, would continue to attract attention, and might be confounded with the Sun God in his form of ' Horus of the Horizon.' It may have been that the cult of Amon was too limited in its appeal to the outlying districts of the Empire, and that this was why the old Heliopolitan sun worship was being revived.

The cult of the Aten which developed from the Heliopolitan sun worship certainly antedated the religious revolution of Akhenaten. A pleasure boat of his father, Amenhotep III, was named 'Aten Gleams,' while the name of the god appears in the name of a palace and even in epithets applied to the king. An even earlier source of the Aten cult is suggested by the veneration for Tuthmosis IV shown by Akhenaten. There seems to have been a shrine of that king in the temple of Aten at Amarna and an ivory carving found there was apparently part of a statue of Tuthmosis. Reference is also made to Tuthmosis IV in a broken part of one of the boundary stelae of the new capital. A curious step toward the invention of the Aten disk is probably to be found in the human arms which are attached to the winged sun disk of Horus on a stela set up at the Sphinx. Although these hold a cartouche of Tuthmosis IV, they suggest the origin of the hands that later form the ends of the life-giving rays that project from the Aten sun disk.

We know little about the reign of Tuthmosis IV. There seems to have been a campaign in Asia, while a close relationship with the kingdom of Mitanni was cemented by the marriage of the king to a daughter of that royal house. It has been suggested that this lady, under her Egyptian name Mutemuya, appears on the monuments as the chief queen and the mother of Amenhotep III, but there seems to be no definite evidence of this. Amenhotep III succeeded to a vast empire which had been kept intact since the conquests of Tuthmosis III, but, except for putting down a revolt in Ethiopia in the fifth year of his reign, he seems scarcely to have exerted himself to maintain his power abroad. He sought to retain his northern vassal princes and allies by means of liberal gifts of Nubian gold. He later neglected even to visit Syria, where the influence of the older generation of princes who had been brought up at the court of Egypt was beginning to wane. The younger men had never seen the king of Egypt, and it is evident from the Tell el Amarna letters, which begin toward the end of the reign of Amenhotep III, that the absence of a show of military force was encouraging energetic men to scheme for independent power and to revolt from Egyptian authority.

The first of a series of large inscribed scarabs commemorates the marriage of Amenhotep to Queen Tiy, a lady of rather obscure origin, judging from the titles of her father and mother. These parents of the queen were buried like royalty in the Valley of the Kings by their son-in-law Amenhotep III, with a magnificent set of funerary equipment. Until the discovery of the Tut-ankh-amon tomb, these beautiful objects in the Cairo Museum gave us our best idea of the furniture of Dynasty XVIII. Other scarabs record a great hunt of wild cattle and ten years of lion hunting, while still another celebrates the completion of a pleasure lake for Queen Tiy at the new palace on the western bank of the Nile, across from Thebes. Gradually Amenhotep seems to have settled back into the indolent and luxurious life of an oriental monarch, concerned solely with the pleasures of his court and the construction of a magnificent series of monuments. To him we owe the Luxor temple with its columned court, which, next to Deir el Bahari, is perhaps the most beautiful of all the buildings of the New Kingdom. The entrance of his enormous funerary temple on the west bank was flanked by the famous colossal seated statues known to the Greeks as the Colossi of Memnon, which are all that now survive of the structure. Other large buildings were erected at Karnak and at other places throughout the country.

Although Tiy retained her position as chief queen and lived on to exert an important influence over her son after Amenhotep's death, the king made other marriages for diplomatic reasons. Like his father, he took as wife a Mitannian princess, Gilukhipa, the daughter of Shuttarna, and towards the end of the reign negotiated another marriage with Tadukhipa the daughter of that king's successor, Tushratta. Amenhotep may have intended this princess for his son to whom she was certainly married after her arrival in Egypt. It is suggested that she is the same person as his beloved Nofretete, but as in the case of Mutemuya this is largely conjectural. Amenhotep III also married the sister of the Kassite ruler of Babylon, and a series of letters refers to the arrangements for his marriage with a second Babylonian princess. The king of Babylon complains that his sister has not been well treated and that none of his messengers has been able to recognize her among the ladies of the court. He also demands an Egyptian princess for himself. In the end he had to be satisfied with a lady of lesser rank, and sent his daughter to be married to Amenhotep III. Similar difficulties were encountered when Amenhotep IV asked for the daughter of the Kassite's successor Burnaburiash. The princess in question died of the plague, and, when a second daughter was ready to go to Egypt in her place, the Babylonian king was insulted that only five chariots had been sent to convey her retinue. The diplomatic correspondence also shows Amenhotep III proposing another alliance by marriage with the Kingdom of Arzawa on the southern coast of Asia Minor.

The growth of the cult of Aten seems to have had little effect on the worship of the other gods until shortly after the accession of the son of Amenhotep III. The fanatical Amenhotep IV instituted a sharp reversal of policy. The main attack was levelled at the priesthood of Amon. The cause of this was probably as much political as religious, for the high priest of the god at Thebes had gained such wealth and power as to be a distinct menace to the throne. We have seen that as early as the reign of Hatshepsut it had been necessary to combine the office of High Priest of Amon with that of the Vizier in the person of one of the queen's devoted followers. Since that time the rich plunder from Tuthmosis III's campaigns and the foreign tribute received during the following reigns had swelled to bursting the coffers of the temple of Amon. Amenhotep IV at first tried to live at Thebes, where he erected a temple to the Aten east of Amon's temple of Karnak. Apparently embittered by the reaction to his reforms in the capital, he soon withdrew from the city and founded a new residence at Tell el Amarna in Middle Egypt. By his sixth year we find that he had erected boundary stelae for his new capital and altered his name from Amenhotep to Akhenaten. He remained at Amarna until his death some eleven years later, scorning to return to Thebes. After the death of Amenhotep III we find the persecution of the hated god Amon carried on systematically throughout the country. Everywhere the name of Amon was erased, even when it occurred in the name of the king's father.

The worship of the creative power of the sun under the name of Aten required no images of the god and was carried out in the open air of the temple court, largely by the placing of flowers and fruit on the altars. If not completely monotheistic, the new cult certainly tended in that direction. Contrary to the old Heliopolitan sun worship upon which it was based, this creed completely neglected the other gods, although they were not persecuted with the zeal which attempted to obliterate all memory of Amon. Far simpler than the old religion, it laid emphasis upon truth, or rather, upon individual liberty. With this was bound up a love of nature, for the life-giving powers of the sun were universally expressed in all living things. In contrast to the old beliefs, largely funerary, which involved a recognition of good and evil, there was little concern with moral laws. Interpretation of the new religion was entirely in the hands of the king, who, with the assistance of his family, performed the sacred offices. The hymns composed by the king express above all a spontaneous joy in living and the love for all created things in which the spirit of the Aten is embodied.

At Tell el Amarna, in a sandy plain where the eastern hills make a wide curve away from the river, Akhenaten created a new city which was intended to provide a more congenial background for his religious experiment. Patterned somewhat after his father's palace at Birket Habu in western Thebes, there were rambling palaces and villas surrounded by orchards and gardens pleasantly interspersed with pools and little summer-houses. Gay wall paintings and vines and flowering shrubs concealed the signs of hasty construction. The great temple of the Aten was a series of columned courts surrounded by an enclosing wall and entered by monumental gateways. In the desert cliffs behind the town, tombs were cut for the favorite members of the king's court, while a royal tomb was excavated in a remote valley.

Although the paintings perfectly express the delight in nature which had always been one of the basic elements of Egyptian art and now was receiving full encouragement, the enormous areas to be covered by relief sculpture in palace, temple, and tomb necessitated hasty workmanship. Sunk relief was universally adopted and the new freedom was unfortunately accompanied by somewhat slovenly craftsmanship, not only at Amarna but also in the Aten shrine at Karnak. This is not true of the sculpture in the round. The emphasis upon truth and individuality inspired the sculptor, who had always shown a liking for portraiture, to produce some of the most remarkable heads that were ever made in Egypt. The exaggeration which accompanied the revolutionary action at the beginning of the reign, as it is exemplified in the strange colossal statues of the king at Karnak, was somewhat softened as time went on. It is almost completely absent from the finest sculpture of the period.

It is interesting to see that in the private tombs most of the traditional scenes were replaced by representations of the king and his family. The owner of the tomb appears only in his connections with the king, either receiving favors from him or executing some duty in his service. It is curious that at a time when individual liberties were being preached, all evidence of a man's personal life should be crowded from his tomb by conventionally repeated set-pieces of the royal family. It looks almost as though spontaneity and individualism were thought of as perquisites of the king, rather than as universal blessings. The outward forms of funerary ritual were retained, although altered in certain respects. The sculptors of the royal tomb represented the funeral ceremonies of one of the princesses, while the inner chapels of the private tombs, although in most cases unfinished, were intended to contain scenes of the burial rites.

The Atenist revolution did not survive the death of Akhenaten. His co-regent and successor, Semenkhkara, almost immediately initiated a reconciliation with the followers of Amon, who must have maintained some kind of an underground organization during their persecution by the heretic king. A compromise was reached in which Amon was again recognized, although the king still kept the Aten form of his name (Nefer-neferu-aten). An inscription is dated to the year 3, but Semenkhkara cannot have reigned much longer, and we find him succeeded by the boy Tut-ankh-amon. The latter was about eighteen when he died and is known to have reigned at least nine years, so he must have been very young at his accession. The origin of these two kings is very obscure, although it is possible that they were brothers. Both based their claim to the throne upon their marriage to daughters of Akhenaten. The youth who succeeded Semenkhkara carried forward the policy of re-establishing Amon. He altered his name from Tut-ankh-aten to Tut-ankh-amon, and that of his wife to Ankhes-en-amon. Amarna was abandoned and the residence transferred to Thebes. On his Karnak stela the king deplores the condition of the temples of the gods which had fallen into ruin, and speaks of his work in rebuilding them. But there was hesitation in repudiating Aten, who, in spite of the restoration of Amon, still kept a footing among the gods. This attempt to reconcile the Aten worship with the old religion was to continue through the short reign of Ay, and it was only after Horemheb came to the throne that the persecution of Aten commenced with the same persistence that had formerly been applied to Amon. Semenkhkara, Tut-ankh-amon, and Ay were all included with Akhenaten as heretic kings, and their names, along with that of Aten, were blotted out and replaced by those of Horemheb and Amon.

The Amarna style in art was not so quickly obliterated. It remains strongly evident in the decoration of the furniture of Tut-ankh-amon and in the wall paintings of his tomb and that of Ay, as well as in Tut-ankh-amon's reliefs in the Luxor temple. Perhaps the finest expression of the Amarna style is to be found in the reliefs of the Memphite tomb of Horemheb, erected while he was still a general, probably in the reign of Tut-ankh-amon. While retaining all the freedom of the Amarna school in the realistic treatment of faces and of individual peculiarities, and making full use of the curving lines so characteristic of Akhenaten's draughtsmen, the workmanship is superior to most of the wall reliefs found at Amarna. Not only are the sunk reliefs more neatly carved, but a beautiful low relief of exceptionally fine quality is also used. Traces of the style remain after Horemheb became king, in his Karnak reliefs and in the Nubian triumphal scene at Gebel Silsileh, although these begin to suggest the over-refined, more conventional style of the next dynasty. The influence of Amarna lingered on into Dynasty XIX. It persisted in the flowing curved lines and in the drawing of drapery, but was chiefly apparent in a certain sketchiness of treatment that was to have a disastrous effect upon painting. Occasionally the free treatment of a peasant with his herd of goats in a Theban tomb painting, or the realistic details of a Nubian village or Syrian fortress which enliven the dull expanse of the great battle scenes in the temples, suggest the influence exerted by the sharp observation of the Amarna craftsmen. Such realistic details had occurred, however, in minor positions throughout all Egyptian wall decoration.

In the background of the reigns of Semenkhkara and Tut-ankh-amon were two much more powerful men, the old courtier Ay and the general Horemheb. A fragment of gold leaf shows Tut-ankh-amon sacrificing a Syrian prisoner in the presence of the Divine Father Ay. The young king is accompanied by his queen and perhaps the whole representation should be dismissed as a routine imitation of what might have been a real action of one of Tut-ankh-amon's more war-like forbears. The presence of Ay, however, suggests his influence over the youthful king and queen. The titles borne by Horemheb in his Memphite tomb suggest that he was even more powerful than Ay and was really governing the country. That he was a better administrator than a general is very probable. Tut-ankh-amon admits in his Karnak stela that in the past if an army was sent to Djahi (Phoenicia) to enlarge the frontiers of Egypt, it met with no success, and there is little to show that conditions in the North had improved. Horemheb, during his administration depicted a large group of Asiatics suppliant before the king, but the inscription tells us that these had been driven from their homes and were begging to be allowed to live in Egypt. Northern Syria had certainly been seized by the Hittites, and Horemheb, even after he came to the throne, seems to have been able to maintain only an uncertain hold over Canaan and Southern Syria. Horemheb boasts of a commission which he executed with success in Kush, but the south was already held firmly by the Viceroy Huy, who has left in his tomb an impressive scene of the presentation of Kushite tribute to Tut-ankh-amon.

The premature death of Tut-ankh-amon left no legitimate claimant to the throne of Egypt, and his wife Ankhes-en-amon was probably the widowed queen who took the dangerous course of writing to the Hittite king, begging him to send one of his sons to share her throne as consort. Suppiluliumas was at that moment besieging Carchemish and was extremely suspicious of such a proposal. By the time that he had made up his mind to act, Ay had already seized the throne, apparently with the support of Horemheb. Ay undertook the burial of Tut-ankh-amon, and is pictured on the walls of the tomb officiating at the funeral. It has been suggested that, just as he appropriated the colossal statues of Tut-ankh-amon's funerary temple at Medinet Habu, he really usurped the larger

113

tomb in which he himself was later buried and crowded the young king's magnificent equipment into a small tomb that was standing unused at the time. Ironically enough, the very insignificance of this little tomb saved it from the erasures of Horemheb and the destructive plundering which occurred in Ay's burial place.

Why Horemheb supported Ay is uncertain. Perhaps he did not yet feel strong enough to take drastic action. He could be certain that the old man would not live long to stand in his way, and in fact Ay died after a brief reign of four years. Horemheb came of a line of provincial nobles in a small town in Middle Egypt, but he covered his seizure of the throne by the now familiar expedient of having the image of Amon recognize him as the rightful ruler. His long career as an administrator had enlightened him as to the laxness and political corruption which had increased dangerously since the beginning of Akhenaten's reign. He promptly initiated a widespread series of reforms which were of the utmost benefit to the country. His modification of obsolete laws was particularly designed to benefit the agricultural peasant, whose well-being formed the basis for the prosperity of the country. It was clear to him that the friction caused by religious controversy must be eased, and his persecution of the Aten heresy was a purely political expedient. His practical administrative reforms were of infinitely greater benefit to the country than had been Akhenaten's religious experiment. On the other hand, in restoring the Amon priesthood to power, he again risked the potential danger to the monarchy inherent in that body of ambitious men.

THE ART OF DYNASTY XVIII AS ILLUSTRATED
BY THIS COLLECTION

THE ART of the early New Kingdom forms a logical continuation of that of the Old and Middle Kingdoms. Architecture, sculpture, and painting show an amplification and refinement of forms already established. The architects made skilful use of the polygonal limestone column in the terraces of the Deir el Bahari temple which was inspired to a certain extent by the neighboring structure of King Mentuhotep. The sculptors lengthened the proportions of their statues, producing slender, more elegant versions of Middle Kingdom forms. One is reminded of the crisp, taut, nervous quality that appeared in Dynasty XI when Theban sculpture was rising out of the barbarism of the First Intermediate Period. In the wall paintings, freshness of color and precision in drawing are what impress us. The tonality is light, employing shades of pink, blue, and gray with canary yellow and brick red. The figures are widely spaced and stiffly grouped with a disregard for relationship in space. The neat, sure outlines remind one of the smooth execution in such a statue as the famous standing figure of Tuthmosis III in the Cairo Museum, which has a similar calm reserve, although at the same time suggesting suppressed nervous energy.

Until the end of the reign of Tuthmosis III we can see sculptors, painters, and architects working to perfect this style, which accords well with the Egyptian spirit as we have come to know it through earlier works. Its architectural master-piece is the temple of Deir el Bahari, with that very original scheme of rising terraces so perfectly suited to the magnificent background of cliffs against which it is built. The breadth of the plan reflects the growing splendors of the New Kingdom in contrast to the tighter design of the Middle Kingdom temple which, in part, suggested its form. The buildings of the temple of Karnak, which was beginning to assume its later magnificence, are lacking in architectural unity, while the festival hall which Tuthmosis III built there, with its curious use of columns imitating poles, as though a huge tent had been transformed into stone, strikes one as a less satisfactory design than Deir el Bahari.

The reliefs of Deir el Bahari are as important as the architecture in expressing the spirit of the first half of Dynasty XVIII. They also reflect early prototypes, as in the decoration of the offering room, which bears a remarkable resemblance to the sanctuary of the temple of Pepy II at South Saqqarah. However, the begin-ning of that wider interest in the outer world is vividly illustrated by the realistic details of the African village in the scenes of the Queen's expedition to Punt. This same familiarity with foreign lands is reflected in the private tombs of the reigns of Hatshepsut and Tuthmosis III by the processions of tribute-bearing en-voys, Asiatics, Nubians, and men of the Isles of the Sea. The Hatshepsut reliefs are admirably imitated in the painted carvings of the tomb of Puyemra, who was one of the men concerned with the construction of Deir el Bahari. He utilized architectural details from that great building in his tomb, and probably em-ployed some of its workmen to execute his reliefs.

A few rare statues give us a glimpse of the development of sculpture in the round. Such is the charming, slim little seated figure of the ancestress of the kings of Dynasty XVIII, Teti-sheri, in the British Museum, or, the rather stiff, painted limestone seated statue of Amenhotep I in Turin. These suggest the logi-cal conclusion to be reached in the numerous statues of Hatshepsut from Deir el Bahari or, even better, the Karnak standing figure of Tuthmosis III in Cairo, mentioned above. In painting, the masterpiece of the early period is undoubted-ly the tomb of Tuthmosis' vizier, Rekhmira, which, now that it has been cleaned, displays more fully the clarity of color and admirable design which made it one of the greatest examples of Egyptian painting in the Theban Necropolis.

A change can be seen already in the tomb of Kenamon of the reign of Amen-hotep II, which was made not long after that of Rekhmira and rivals it in beauty. Here a greater richness in coloring and design is evident, a sumptuous effect, both in style and subject matter, which contrasts with the clear-cut purity of tone and outline, the severity, of the earlier tombs. There is no doubt that a new spirit prevailed at the close of the reign of Tuthmosis III, making itself felt in all branches of art. The old simplicity and straightforwardness of attack is gone, and with them something of value is lost, although the loss is not so clearly felt in the midst of the surge of new influences, the superficial glitter of wealth and splendor. Egypt was beginning to show the effect of its conquests abroad. It is not so much in the employment of foreign motifs that outside influence made itself felt, for, after all, such adaptation remained a superficial element. It is rather the widening of the Egyptian's outlook, the consciousness of being a power in a vaster world than he had hitherto imagined. The result of this realization was ostentation, a desire to display all the new wealth, a tendency toward the grandiose and the colossal which was to grow steadily with the waning dynasty and on into the following period. Fundamentally one has the feeling that the growth of the Empire was not beneficial to the Egyptian and in many ways corrupted his art. The continuity is interrupted and, beginning with the reign of Amenhotep II, new elements are substituted which are not well adjusted to the rhythm of the native character.

In this collection, the wooden statuette of a king, from Kerma, (Fig. 57) has already been mentioned in discussing the objects of the late Middle Kingdom. Although certainly to be dated earlier, probably at a time just previous to the Hyksos invasion, it seems to anticipate the slender proportions and new spirit of Dynasty XVIII. From the reign of Hatshepsut several objects vividly recall important events in that woman's brilliant career. Two fragments of red granite (Nos. 75.12, 13) formed part of that one of her two Karnak obelisks which now lies broken on the ground. The transportation and erection of these great shafts had been commemorated by Hatshepsut as being only secondary in importance to her famous expedition to Punt. One of our fragments is a corner piece from the lower part of the shaft. Part of the large hieroglyphs of an inscription which ran down the center are preserved, flanked by a figure of the god Amon. On the adjoining face, which was the north side of the obelisk, is a similar figure of the god to whom the obelisks and temple were dedicated. The second fragment probably also came from the north face of the shaft. It is one of the series of royal figures which stand one above the other, facing representations of Amon on the other side of the central line of vertical inscription. Although Hatshepsut represented both her father and Tuthmosis III among these figures, it is probable that in this case we have the queen herself, dressed as a man and wearing the double crown of Upper and Lower Egypt (Fig. 67).

The beautifully carved sunk relief of the figures on the obelisk fragments is an excellent example of the precise, clean-cut workmanship of early Dynasty XVIII and closely resembles the style of the decoration on the coffin of Tuthmosis I (Fig. 68). This rectangular quartzite box with the royal cartouche encircling the top surface of the lid had been prepared originally for Hatshepsut herself, as has been described on page 105. Probably before the coffin ever left the workshop, the queen decided to transfer her father's burial to her tomb and to prepare another sarcophagus for herself. The interior of the box had to be enlarged, while all the inscriptions were altered to substitute the king's name for that of Hatshepsut. On both the outer and inner surfaces, the ends of the coffin show kneeling figures of Isis and Nephthys, the bereaved sisters of Osiris, who attend the king as wailing women when he takes the form of that god. The side panels are carved with the figures of the four genii of the dead, and the jackal-headed Anu-bis. Appropriate texts from the Book of the Dead accompany these sunk relief figures, as well as an inscription announcing the preparation of the coffin for the queen's father. A figure of the sky goddess Nut appears on the floor of the box as well as on both the upper and lower surfaces of the lid.

The foundation deposits of that tomb of Hatshepsut in which her father's cof-fin was placed consist of small vessels of alabaster, bearing the queen's name, and similar vessels of red pottery (No. 05.66, etc.). With these were placed wo-ven rush trays, tiny model mats of rushes, pieces of linen, and various tools, as well as a wooden mould for brick-making which bears the name of Hatshepsut.

67. Queen Hatshepsut from her broken Karnak obelisk

117

68. Sarcophagus of Tuthmosis I

Similar objects were placed in the foundation deposits of the Deir el Bahari temple, of which we also have a representative collection (No. 95.1414, etc.). Perhaps the most interesting piece is a wooden model of a rocker for moving heavy masonry blocks (No. 95.1410). It is a kind of sledge with curved runners and is inscribed with the name of the queen. Of the other objects, a large wooden adze with a metal blade is a practicable tool rather than a model.

A hound attacking a pink gazelle is sketched on a flake of limestone from the tomb of Hatshepsut's favorite minister, Senmut. The animated movement of these figures began to appear in the hunting scenes of the early New Kingdom for which this was evidently a preliminary study (Fig. 86).

The painted limestone architrave from Abydos (No. 02.861) is a good example of the decorative use of hieroglyphs in the building inscriptions of Tuthmosis III. We are fortunate in possessing one of the very important historical monuments of this greatest of Egyptian conquerors. This is the granite stela found by Dr. Reisner in the Temple of Amon at Gebel Barkal, the Sacred Mountain near

118

Napata, the capital of Kush (Ethiopia) (No. 23.733). The inscription corroborates the account of Tuthmosis' Asiatic campaigns, found more completely described in the king's Karnak Annals. In addition to a description of the Battle of Megiddo there is recorded a lesser event, the elephant hunt at Niy, which is known elsewhere only from the king's Erment stela and the tomb of General Amenemhab. The inscription closes with a tantalizingly brief reference to the observation of the miraculous movement of a star. Tuthmosis III is also represented in the collection by a seated statuette (No. 23.737) from Gebel Barkal. Unfortunately it is broken away above the waist, but suggests the same crisp carving and youthful energy that appear in other more complete versions of the king's statue.

The early kings of Dynasty XVIII strengthened the defenses of the Middle Kingdom fortresses which guarded the passage to Ethiopia through the difficult region of the Second Cataract. At Semna there was a fort on each side of the river in which the Tuthmosid family built small temples with polygonal columns and reliefs like those at Thebes. From the Eastern Fort (Kumma) come the standstone sunk reliefs showing Tuthmosis III making offerings to the ram-headed Khnum (No. 25.1510; Fig. 69). These blocks had been discarded and built into the lower

69. Relief of Tuthmosis III from Temple in Cataract fort at Kumma

70. Faience jar and shawabtis from the tomb of Tuthmosis IV

part of a wall during alterations of the time of Amenhotep II, perhaps undertaken by the Viceroy Weser-satet (see p. 108). The granite rocks near the forts bear
many inscriptions offering prayers to the gods, or recording a successful expedition, made by the men who passed back and forth through this desolate region
on the king's business. Similar mementos are the two round-topped stelae of the
Viceroy Weser-satet erected at Semna, one of which is dated in the year 23, of
the reign of Amenhotep II (Nos. 25.632, 633). The rather dreary life of the wives
of the garrison officers must have been brightened by occasional gifts of jewelry
and beautifully worked toilet articles. Among such prized possessions were the
amethyst and carnelian necklaces and the bronze counterweight with a head of
the goddess Hathor which hung down at the back of the neck to balance a heavy
collar (No. 29.1199). From Semna came also the charming bronze mirror with
the handle in the form of a naked girl (No. 29.1197) and another which has its
wooden handle carved in the shape of the grotesque little lion-headed Bes, the
god of the toilet (No. 29.1198). Another bronze mirror, of uncertain origin, is
supported by a Nubian girl who holds a tiny duck to her breast (Fig. 72). From
Egypt itself came the small green-glazed jar for eye-paint with its lively frieze of
animals (No. 00.701). The small ibis, with feathers formed by dark blue paste
fused into gold cloisons, is a magnificent example of New Kingdom metal work
(Fig. 71), although its exact date and place of origin are uncertain.

The growing magnificence of the second half of Dynasty XVIII is well represented by the equipment of the tomb of Tuthmosis IV from which we have a

71. Inlaid gold ibis

72. Bronze mirror

73. Wooden panther from tomb of Tuthmosis IV

74. Cairo statuette of Tut-ankh-amon to suggest use of panther (DRAWING BY SUZANNE E. CHAPMAN)

large number of objects. Perhaps the finest of these is a striding panther carved from wood and covered with pitch (Fig. 73). The lithe movement of the animal can be seen to advantage in the present simplicity of the incomplete piece. Unfortunately we know from the tomb of Tut-ankh-amon that the original composition was clumsily ornate. The panther formed the support for a gilded statuette of the king which was perched upon its back (see the drawing, Fig. 74). The delicately carved wooden panel is a companion piece to an almost identical carving in the Metropolitan Museum. They formed the arms of a chair like one from the tomb of Tut-ankh-amon or that of the parents of Queen Tiy. The drawing, Fig. 75, shows our panel restored as the arm-rest of such a chair as appears frequently in tomb scenes showing the king in his audience chamber. One side of the

75. Suggested restoration of chair with Tuthmosis IV arm panel (DRAWING BY
SUZANNE E. CHAPMAN)

panel (Fig. 75) shows the king as a sphinx trampling on prostrate Asiatics, a favorite subject which goes back to Old Kingdom reliefs. On the other side, Thoth and a lion-headed goddess offer the enthroned king a reign of millions of years. Similarly carved, and probably originally gilded, is the upper part of the wooden piece which once held the ostrich feathers of a fan (No. 03.1132). Such fan holders are common in the paintings of the New Kingdom and complete examples were found in Tut-ankh-amon's tomb.

Of the more ordinary objects found in the tomb of Tuthmosis IV, by far the most attractive are the vessels, models, and funerary figures of faience covered with a brilliant, deep blue glaze, with inscriptions and designs in black (Fig. 70). The vases are covered with characteristic New Kingdom patterns composed of lotus and papyrus flowers, a feather or scale design, and geometric forms. Faience models of throwing sticks, papyrus rolls, and large *ankh*-signs, symbols of life, were also placed in the tomb, as well as small servant figures, called shawabtis, which were intended to undertake all labors for the dead in the Underworld. While one of the limestone Canopic jars (No. 03.1130) probably came from a set of four belonging to the king, the other (No. 03.1129) is inscribed with the name of Prince Amenemhat, who was probably a son of Tuthmosis IV. Each jar has its lid in the form of the head of one of the four genii of the dead which are represented on the coffin of Tuthmosis I.

Even more graceful than the faience vessels from this royal tomb are the bronze and colored faience cups and vases from private tombs, several of which are exhibited. The slender, long necked vessels are particularly characteristic of the New Kingdom as are the lotus goblets with their high stems. A blue-glazed rhyton, although certainly of Egyptian workmanship, has been copied from the Aegean 'filler' used for pouring liquids. The form is familiar to us from the silver rhyton carried by the cup-bearer in the Knossos fresco and appears among the gifts brought by the Cretan envoys in the Theban tombs of the first half of Dynasty XVIII. Other examples of many-colored faience, the fragmentary tall-necked vase with lotus patterns (No. 05.191) and the Hathor heads (Nos. 05.176, 178), come from the temple of that goddess at the turquoise mines in the Sinai Peninsula.

One of the few private persons to be buried in the Valley of the Kings was a contemporary of Amenhotep II, the Fan-bearer Mai-her-peri. A piece of his linen mummy wrappings bore the cartouche of Hatshepsut, but the style of the objects in the tomb suggests that this linen was used at a later date than that at which the queen's name was marked on it. The tomb produced many beautiful things which are now in the Cairo Museum. Just outside the entrance was buried a small yellow box inscribed with the name of Mai-her-peri (No. 03.1036), which contained two remarkable examples of leather-working. These were loincloths of intricately cut gazelle skin. One of them is in this collection (Fig. 76). The garment was tied around the waist with the plain square surface of leather in the back, while the rounded projection was drawn between the legs and fastened at

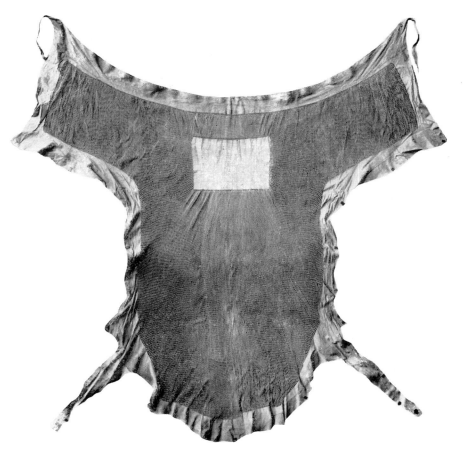

76. Cut skin garment of Mai-her-peri

77. Man wearing garment like Fig. 76

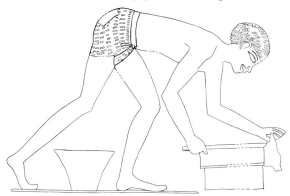

the waist in front. Except for the border and the rectangular "patch," the whole surface is composed of fine crisscross threads of skin formed by cutting out infinitesimal squares from the leather. That this could have been done with such precision and regularity seems almost impossible, but the strands have been spliced only in a few places. Similar garments are often seen worn by workmen in Theban tomb paintings (Fig. 77), sometimes apparently to protect their linen kilts. However, such a delicately worked piece as this must have been more ornamental than serviceable. Stains of wear show that it was not made expressly for the tomb.

The statuette of Amenhotep III found in the temple of Gebel Barkal betrays little of the style of the second half of Dynasty XVIII (No. 23.734). It is much more reminiscent of the severe treatment characteristic of the statues of Tuthmosis III. In distant Kush the agents of Akhenaten erased the hated name of Amon in the king's cartouche. Even if the face of this statue were preserved we probably should not find in it a hint of the curious expression that appears in the brown quartzite head (Fig. 78) which is probably to be attributed to Amenhotep III because of its resemblance to a large head of the king in the British Museum. The drawing up of the corners of the mouth into an enigmatic smile, and the pronounced use of curved lines where the rather flat facial planes join, lend an exotic quality to this head which is in keeping with the character of that luxury loving monarch. The elegance of the costume of the period as well as feminine charm are to be found at their best in the dark stone statuette of a court lady (Fig. 80). The thin pleated robe clinging to the body and the elaborately curled wig are carved with the greatest delicacy. The same attention to the details of costume and hairdressing is to be found in three pieces of limestone sculpture, the upper part of the figure of a man in a fringed robe (No. 09.526), the head of a man (No. 97.889), and a woman's head (No. 11.1483).

The granite shawabti of Amenhotep III is a very large example of one of these funerary figures and, contrasted with the smaller shawabtis of Tuthmosis IV executed in the comparatively cheap glazed faience, is an indication of the wealth lavished upon all the products of this extravagant reign (No. 04.1854). The impressive seated statue of the goddess Sekhmet in dark stone (Fig. 81) is representative of the temple sculpture of the time. It was one of many such figures which lined the court of the temple of Mut erected by Amenhotep III south of the Amon temple at Karnak. These lion-headed female figures must have been grimly effective standing in long rows against the walls. As usual, the Atenists have mutilated the cartouches of the king to destroy the mention of Amon. The granite head (Fig. 79) closely resembles the features of the scribe statues of the king's favorite minister, Amenhotep, Son of Hapu. The large scarab (No. 04. 1810) records the slaying of one hundred and two lions in the first ten years after the king's accession to the throne. It represents a custom of commemorating memorable events by an issue of such scarabs, which was peculiar to the reign of Amenhotep III. The two sandstone walls of the chapel of the Treasurer Sebek-

78. Amenhotep III

79. Granite head

mose are cut in sunk relief of the style of the reign of Amenhotep III. One wall has an interesting representation of a New Kingdom funeral while the other shows the tomb owner pouring ointment on a figure of the god of the dead, Anubis (Fig. 82).

Since several of the magnificent tombs of the courtiers of this time were carved in the better limestone at the foot of the Qurneh hill, the sculptors were able to employ reliefs again in their wall decorations. From one of these tombs comes a small piece of characteristic low relief. The soldiers with shields strapped over their shoulders are evidently bowing before the king in respectful greeting (Fig. 83). In the remarkable copies of Mr. Joseph Lindon Smith we can study the details from the finest of all these tombs, that of the Vizier Ramose. Here the draughtsman made an increasing use of curved lines and excelled in the graceful representation of pleated garments and voluminous wigs. The low modelling is very fine while the outlines of the faces are especially delicate. Firmness and clarity of drawing prevent the minutely observed detail from becoming confused or the modelling from appearing over soft. In the funeral scene where little relief had been completed we find the painter rivalling the sculptor. A new element here is the expressive gestures and grouping of the wailing women. The artist has even shown tears trickling down their cheeks.

The decoration of the tomb of Ramose was commenced in the last years of the reign of Amenhotep III and is very important as providing an abrupt contrast to the official art of that time in a wall which was commenced after his son's advent to power. Here suddenly we find the new art of Amenhotep IV in all the peculiarities of the style of the first few years of his revolution while he still resided at Thebes. If one compares the figure of Ramose on this wall in Mr. Smith's copy

with any of the older figures in the tomb one senses at once the immense difference in feeling that has intervened. Here is the subservient bowed figure so familiar from the Amarna reliefs, the same exaggerated use of curved lines and the
pronounced distortion of the skull which gives all the people of Akhenaten's family and court the appearance of having a cranial deformation. The work on this
part of the wall was never carried beyond the masterly drawing of the scene of
the king's audience to foreign ambassadors. Before the reliefs could be executed
the court had moved to the new capital at Tell el Amarna.

80. Statuette of a lady

Opposite: 81. The Goddess Sekhmet

82. Sebekmose offering to Anubis

83. Soldiers greeting Amenhotep III

At Amarna the sculptors showed a partiality for sunk relief. We have in our collection a number of characteristic examples. These are sculptor's trial pieces, fragments of stelae, or parts of the wall decoration of the great palace, and come from the excavations of the Egypt Exploration Society. Although the extreme style of the first few years disappeared to a great extent in the statues, it continued unabated in the reliefs, particularly in the stelae and, as is not surprising, in the trial sketches which were swiftly chiselled out on flakes of limestone. A good example of such a sketch is the small piece (No. 37.2) where the back of the head is indicated only by an incised line, whereas nose, mouth, and chin are carefully modelled. Another (No. 36.95) is a more finished study. Fig. 84 shows the head and raised arms of a royal figure, probably Akhenaten rather than Queen Nofretete. The face has the haggard, elongated treatment and pendulous jaw found in all the figures of the boundary stelae which Akhenaten carved on the desert cliffs to delimit the area of his new capital. This limestone fragment is thought to come from the right side of Stela P which was long ago blown up with gunpowder by treasure hunters. The royal couple once stood with uplifted arms praising the disk of the Aten, one of whose rays holds out the sign of life to the king's nostrils.

With its emphasis upon the informal family life of the king, the Amarna sculpture abounds in representations of the little princesses. These, whether in the round or in relief, show the physical distortions imposed by the new style in its least happy form. The enormously projecting bald skulls and hanging jaws appear characteristically in the quartzite relief (No. 39.58) and in the granite

84. Akhenaten worshipping the Aten

85. Head of a princess from Amarna

86. Painted sketch of hound attacking gazelle. Early Dyn. XVIII, from tomb of Senmut (see p. 118)

fragment (No. 34.49). In these baby princesses the Amarna craftsmen captured the immature forms of childhood in a manner new to Egyptian art which had always shown children as miniature replicas of grown-up persons. In a little head from the wall decorations of one of the columned halls of the palace the delicate, rather melancholy charm that pervades so much of the Amarna work is seen at its best (Fig. 85). The realism which underlies the stylistic peculiarities of the time makes itself strongly felt in two other fragments (Nos. 39.56 and 37.4).

The gaiety of the Amarna paintings as well as that happy interest in all the forms of nature appears in the delightfully colored fluttering pigeons and ducks, the thistles and swamp plants of the fragments of glazed tiles that lined one of the rooms of the great palace (Nos. 37.12, 13, and 16 to 18). Equally bright and charming are the faience necklace elements and amulets in the shape of pomegranates, flower petals, bunches of grapes, thistle heads, and a variety of other forms which were manufactured in such quantities at the new capital (No. 36.98, etc.). The same liveliness is to be found in the lions and dogs attacking calves on the exquisitely carved toilet box (Fig. 87) which has been dated to the reign of Tut-ankh-amon. Equally characteristic of the small carvings of the mid-Eighteenth Dynasty is the tiny dwarf carrying a jar (Fig. 89). The wooden toilet spoon (Fig. 88) was found by our expedition in a New Kingdom cemetery in the Memphite region. It so closely resembles a piece in the Brooklyn Museum from a nearby site and dated to the Amarna Period that it may well come from the same workshop. The container is in the form of a duck which has been captured by a naked swimming girl whose hair is elaborately braided.

The influence of Amarna is strong in the sculpture of the following reigns, even after Tut-ankh-amon had returned to Thebes. To this time probably belongs the sandstone head (Fig. 90) which resembles so closely the gold mummy mask of Tut-ankh-amon and his granite statue in Cairo that it can probably be safely assigned to that king. It is very probable that the fragment of sunk relief (Fig. 91) comes from the side of the throne of one of the colossal statues now in Berlin and Cairo which were usurped by Horemheb from the Pharaoh Ay. Ay had himself appropriated two large standing figures of Tut-ankh-amon in the temple at Medinet Habu which was commenced by that young king, so it is not

87. Toilet box with leaping animals. Late Dyn. XVIII

88. Wooden toilet spoon

89. Small wooden dwarf with vase

90. Head of Tut-ankh-amon

impossible that these seated figures from the same place were also originally made for Tut-ankh-amon. The relief fragment is identical in style with, and almost certainly fits, a larger piece found during the excavations of the Oriental Institute. It also resembles a piece sketched long ago by Lepsius. It shows the upper part of a Nile god tying together the plants of Upper and Lower Egypt, a familiar form of heraldry for the decoration of a throne basis. It is a beautiful example of the relief sculpture of the close of Dynasty XVIII.

91. Nile god from throne of statue of Ay

THE HISTORICAL BACKGROUND: DYNASTY XIX

HOREMHEB had shown great favors to an army officer named Pa-ramesses whom he made Vizier. Ramesses' family came from the city of Tanis in the Delta where the worship of the god Seth had been kept alive since Hyksos times. He was the son of the Chief of the Archers, Sety. Already an old man when he succeeded to the throne at the death of Horemheb, Ramesses I only reigned two years. He was really the founder of the family of Dynasty XIX, although Horemheb is often placed as the first of its kings. There seems to have been no actual relationship between Horemheb and Ramesses. The new family remained faithful to the place of its origin and made Tanis the summer capital. Ramesses' son Sety I had distinguished himself under Horemheb and bore important military titles when his father made him co-regent. He was the first of a line of warriors who turned all their efforts toward recovering Egypt's prestige abroad. It must be remembered, though, that the campaigns of Sety I, Ramesses II, and Merenptah were based upon the prosperity resulting from the wise interior policy developed by Horemheb.

No sooner had Ramesses died than the Shasu Bedouin broke out in revolt on the very borders of Egypt. Far more serious was a Syrian coalition formed along much the same lines as that which had faced Tuthmosis III, but this time encouraged by the Hittites instead of the now vanished kingdom of Mitanni. Sety was fortunately able to attack the different members of the coalition piecemeal before they had time to join forces, and soon regained control over Palestine. Sety apparently patterned his military undertakings upon the campaigns of Tuthmosis III. After repulsing a Libyan attack, we find him in northern Syria where Egyptian troops for the first time came into actual contact with the Hittites. The policy of maintaining peace with Egypt, which had continued under the reign of the Hittite King Mursilis, came to an end with his death, and it was probably his son, Muwatallis, who had stirred up the rebellion in Palestine. Sety I managed to capture Kadesh, but, though the Hittites were forced to retire temporarily, they retained their influence in North Syria. The war was to be continued by Ramesses II and end finally in a stalemate between the two great powers.

Sety I undertook the construction commenced by his father of the Hypostyle Hall at Karnak, one of the wonders of the ancient world. It is on the outside of the northern wall of this hall that his foreign wars are represented. The enormous columned construction was finished by his son, Ramesses II. Ramesses also completed another important building of his father's, the temple at Abydos. The reliefs of Sety I in this building are probably the most beautiful and certainly the best preserved of all the temple reliefs of the New Kingdom. They are in very smoothly modelled low relief of exceptionally delicate quality. Although difficult to equal for technical excellence, they begin to show a certain over-refinement. They are the last great product of the genius of the Egyptians for relief sculpture. The work that followed them at the Ramesseum or in the great rock-

cut temple at Abu Simbel was coarser in quality and largely executed in sunk relief, as were the remarkable decorations of the Medinet Habu temple of Ramesses III. The Kushite kings employed raised relief, but this was less fine, while the
vast walls of Ptolemaic temples display little more than empty conventionality.
Only in a few Theban tombs at the close of Dynasty XXV and in some smaller
works of a later time does the skill of the Egyptian sculptor in relief again make
itself felt.

The Hittite King Muwatallis formed a coalition against the young Ramesses
II which was stronger than anything the Egyptians had ever faced. It included
not only Northern Syria, but also allies drawn from amongst the peoples of the
Aegean. Ramesses began in the traditional manner by securing the Syrian coast,
where he carved a monument at the Nahr-el-Kelb (Dog River) near Beirut in
his fourth year. In the next year he advanced into the valley of the Orontes and
had almost reached Kadesh when he came upon some Bedouin spies, sent out by
the Hittite king for that purpose, who informed him that the enemy had retired
to the north in the direction of Aleppo. Without waiting for the last two divisions of his army, which were far behind, Ramesses pushed on in pursuit, leaving the second division to follow him at some distance. The Hittite king had
drawn his army into concealment behind Kadesh and, when Ramesses ap-
proached the town, he crossed the river Orontes, keeping the town between himself and the unsuspecting first division of the Egyptian forces. Ramesses set up
camp to the northeast of Kadesh and here he learned from some captives of the
dangerous proximity of the overwhelming force of the enemy. Before he could
act, the Hittite chariotry attacked and routed the second division of his army, the
fleeing troops throwing his own camp into confusion. Had it not been for the
quick action and personal bravery of the Pharaoh, who, with a small band of
household troops, cut his way through one flank of the enemy chariots, the dis-
aster would have been complete. While the Hittites were plundering the camp, a
reinforcement of auxiliaries joined the Egyptians and with these Ramesses was
able to recapture the camp. At this point the third division of the army was
brought up by the vizier, who at the beginning of the battle had been sent off
post-haste to fetch them. These new forces turned the battle in favor of the
Egyptians and the Hittites were forced to retire behind the gates of Kadesh.

However, Ramesses was unable to take Kadesh and withdrew, leaving the Hittites still in possession of the northern country. The Hittite advance was checked
but hostilities continued, nonetheless. Two years later a revolt was fomented in
Palestine. Ramesses stormed Askalon, and continued on into the north to take
other important cities such as Satouna, Dapour, and Tunip. The fighting in Syria
must have continued for a number of years. Tunip, for example, had to be taken
more than once. It was not until his twenty-first year that Ramesses finally con-
cluded a peace by signing a remarkable treaty with the Hittite king Hattusilis.
The latter had succeeded not only to the throne of Muwatallis but to numerous
internal difficulties increased by the threat of Assyria's growing power. The

treaty is preserved on the walls of two Egyptian temples as well as in a cuneiform copy on clay tablets found in the records of the ' Foreign Office ' of the Hittite capital at Boghaz-köi. The two kings undertook reciprocal obligations to come to each other's defense if attacked by a third power, and also arranged for the extradition of political refugees.

By this agreement, Egyptian influence seems to have extended along the coast to the North Syrian town of Ugarit (Ras Shamra), but the Hittites still retained their power in the interior, in the valley of the Orontes. Ramesses II reigned on for forty-six years after signing the treaty. He married a daughter of Hattusilis and peace was maintained with the Hittites. A late story tells us how, at the request of the Hittite king, Ramesses despatched a statue of Khonsu for the purpose of healing a princess who was possessed of a demon. This reminds us of conditions of an earlier day when the image of Ishtar of Assur was sent by the king of Mitanni to cure the aged Amenhotep III. But the power of the Hittites was nearing its close. At the death of Hattusilis a crisis arose in Khatti which was probably due to the first shock of the movement of the Sea Peoples. This great mass migration radiated from the Balkans and the Black Sea region throughout the eastern Mediterranean world, and soon overwhelmed the Hittite kingdom. The king of Assyria promptly took advantage of these troubles of his enemy to overrun Babylonia. The aging Ramesses apparently neglected these ominous signs from abroad, and his vigorous successor, Merenptah, found himself faced with a serious situation when he came to the throne.

The Sea Peoples had filtered into Libya, as they had everywhere along the southern shores of the Mediterranean. Finding this a peculiarly barren land, it was only natural that they should spill over into fertile Egypt. Merenptah met them in a great battle in the western Delta where he inflicted an overwhelming defeat upon the invaders. For about thirty years there was no further trouble from this direction. A triumphal stela, in which for the first time mention is made of Israel, seems to support other evidence that Merenptah also conducted a campaign in Palestine. Merenptah's death resulted in a dynastic struggle which was carried on through the reigns of a succession of five weak pharaohs who largely undid the good work of the three strong kings who had preceded them. Order was restored by Sety-nekht, who seized the throne to reign for a brief two years as the first king of Dynasty XX.

DYNASTY XX

SETY-NEKHT was succeeded by the last great king of the New Kingdom, Ramesses III. He reorganized the administration and the army, and was thus prepared to meet the shocks of two dangerous invasions of the country. Palestine was the last barrier to the main forces of the Sea Peoples which had swept down over the fallen Hittite kingdom and engulfed all Syria. The Delta had received an infiltration of desert Bedouins and refugees from Canaan, while the indigenous inhabitants of Libya, as well as the more recent northern settlers, had drifted in from the west. All these people, with their close foreign affiliations, were a source of anarchy in the richest province of Egypt. In the year 5 a great revolt broke out in Libya. Ramesses had attempted to impose upon the Libyans a young prince of their race who had been brought up in Egypt. The immediate result was a large scale invasion of the Delta. The prompt action of the king brought about a great victory for his troops, near the Canopic branch of the Nile. Three years later the combined forces of the northern sea-faring tribes bore down upon Egypt both by land, through Palestine, and by sea. They were driven off in two great land and naval engagements. The invading forces were permanently deflected from Egypt, one of the groups, the Peleseth (Philistines), settling along the coast of Palestine. In the year 11, a renewal of the Libyan attack, brought on by Mesh-wesh invaders, was beaten off, this time so disastrously that there was never again an organized attack from the west. Ramesses seems to have made some attempt also to regain his Asiatic possessions, but with the Philistines along the coast the Egyptian power was largely limited to the back country of Palestine.

That Ramesses III had restored prosperity to the country is evident enough from such monuments as his funerary temple at Medinet Habu. More important, he had saved his country from being swallowed up, like its great rival, Khatti, by the invasion. Small was the reward returned by his ungrateful subjects. A plot directed against the king by the vizier at Athribis was indeed crushed, but the end of the reign saw a palace conspiracy which originated in the royal harîm. The resulting trial shows the rottenness of the structure which was being held together by the king's own personal ability. A plan to murder the king was instigated by one of the queens, who saw her son displaced from the accession. When a group of important people was brought to trial, several judges were caught drinking and conspiring with the accused and had to be transferred to the criminal's bench. The internal strife brought to light by the court proceedings was to prove only too common throughout the rest of the dynasty.

Decadence set in completely with the following kings, Ramesses IV to XI. Incessant family strife was coupled with low Niles and bad harvests during the reigns of Ramesses VII and his successors, until men spoke of the ' year of the hyenas when one was hungry.' Palestine and Syria were completely lost. Toward the end of the reign of Ramesses IX, thieves broke into the royal tombs and the investigation of the robberies betrays the corruption of the local officials. This state of affairs grew steadily worse until, in Dynasty XXI, it became necessary to remove the bodies of the great pharaohs to a secret cache at Deir el Bahari, where they were found in modern times.

The feeble hold of the royal house was made still more precarious by the growth of power in the hands of the High Priest of Amon. The incumbent of this office under Ramesses XI, Amenhotep, was guilty of such a terrible offense, probably an attempt to seize the throne, that he was suspended. Insurrection in Middle Egypt made necessary the recall of the Viceroy of Ethiopia, Pa-nehesy, who in turn, when he had crushed the rebellion, held dangerous power in his

141

hands. He was replaced by Herihor, who became not only High Priest of Amon but Viceroy of Ethiopia and Vizier. While he relinquished the vizierate after a time, he retained the other two offices, and in the inscriptions of the Khonsu temple at Karnak we find Herihor appearing side by side with the king as joint author of the work. Gradually the king's name disappears in the later stages of the work until Herihor finally assumes the royal titles for himself. His power seems to have been limited to the South, for a man named Smendes was governing as vizier in the North.

RAMESSIDE ART IN THIS COLLECTION

THE POMPOUS GRANDEUR of Ramesside official art makes its impact upon the beholder by the scale of its architecture and statuary, and by the complicated scenes in relief which cover enormous wall surfaces. Since the rather coarsely executed details are subordinated to the vigour of the design and general impressiveness of the whole, the fragments which can be exhibited in museums lose in effectiveness by being separated from their background more than at any earlier period in Egyptian art. Thus, for example, the head of a Libyan, broadly treated in very deep sunk relief (Fig. 92), was meant to be seen high up on a temple wall among hundreds of other figures and against the movement of a great battle scene, or in a procession of foreign captives. It had to be treated simply in order

92. Temple relief with Libyan

93. Red jasper inlay of Sety I

to carry at a distance. The clarity of the representation was also enhanced originally by the use of a few simple tones of brilliant color. The covering of such vast
wall surfaces must often have discouraged the workmen from attempting to execute fine detail, although this was certainly not the case in many parts of the
temple of Medinet Habu. Similarly, in the statues the workmanship of the individual parts might be hastily executed as long as an imposing effect could be
gained. The conventional large seated figure of Ramesses II (No. 87.111), from
Tell Nebesheh in the Delta, must have been one of a succession of such statues,
standing perhaps between the great columns of a temple court such as we can
still see in the temple of Luxor.

At no other period was so great a use made of material usurped from earlier
monuments. Such is the granite shaft with its palm capital from Heracleopolis
bearing the names of Ramesses II and Merenptah (Fig. 43), the large papyrus
bundle-column (Fig. 44) and the Hathor capital from Bubastis (Fig. 46). The
polished dark stone seated figure (No. 88.748) has been usurped by one of the
sons of Ramesses II, Prince Mentu-her-khopeshef, while the Tell Nebesheh
Sphinx made originally for a Middle Kingdom king (No. 88.747), has undergone
numerous alterations of its inscriptions and now bears the names of Ramesses
III and Sety-nekht. It was at the height of this plundering of statues and stone
for building materials that Ramesses II sent his architect to strip the granite from
the Giza pyramid temples. This man has left a proud inscription on the rock wall
behind the Second Pyramid as though he were engaged in a respectable quarrying expedition.

As has been suggested on a preceding page, the work of the reign of Sety I at the beginning of Dynasty XIX is of a different character from that which followed it. The paintings in a private tomb such as that of Userhet have a magnificent decorative effect that has not given way to the sketchy, somewhat slovenly treatment of the figures which soon became so prevalent. We have a copy by Mr. Lindon Smith of part of the group of Userhet and his wife seated beneath a sycamore tree, which forms one of the most beautiful walls in the Theban Necropolis (No. 12.322). A similar subject appears upon a small Dynasty XIX stela from Giza, where the Goddess Hathor is shown emerging from her sycamore tree to dispense food and drink to the dead man and his family assembled beneath (Fig. 94).

The reliefs of Sety I in his temple at Abydos, as at Karnak and in his tomb in the Valley of the Kings, show the most masterly craftsmanship. If one compares Mr. Lindon Smith's copies of some of the finest of the Abydos reliefs with those of details from the tomb of Ramose, it will be seen how much of the refined elegance of the reign of Amenhotep III carried over into early Dynasty XIX. The same clear-cut profile of Sety I, with its aquiline nose, appears again in a tiny jasper face modelled with the utmost delicacy (Fig. 93). This little inlay formed part of a figure of the king evidently made up of various precious materials. Carved in sunk relief of more conventional quality, but reflecting the same style, which verges on over-refinement, is the head of a king (No. 87.663). It came from a part of the temple at Tell Nebesheh which was built by Ramesses II, and probably represents that Pharaoh.

Two viziers of Ramesses II are represented in this collection. A squatting statue of one, Pa-ra-hotep, found at Abydos, shows the man with his arms folded

94. Funerary stela from Giza. Dyn. XIX

95. Stela of the Vizier Paser

on his knees (No. 03.1891). The other is shown on a funerary stela which bears an interesting portrait of the Pharaoh (Fig. 95). Paser, in his long vizier's robe and carrying a feather fan, is being presented to Ramesses II, who, wearing the battle helmet and a flowing pleated robe with wide sleeves, sits upon a cushioned chair. Behind the king stands the goddess Hathor. The face of the king is like that of his father Sety I, a resemblance that is also evident in the well-preserved mummies of the two men. This well-cut limestone stela, with its marked funerary character, may well have come from Paser's tomb at Thebes, in which there is a frequently reproduced scene of artists at work on royal statues.

The magnificent jewelry of the New Kingdom appears heavier in design and coloring than do the brilliant productions of the Middle Kingdom jewelers. Handsome as are the jewels of Tut-ankh-amon, they seem ornate and cumbersome beside the marvelous lightness and delicacy of the Dahshur and Lahun crowns and pectorals. In the same way, we feel that the ornament of the furniture is excessive when it is placed beside that of Queen Hetep-heres I of Dynasty IV. In a smaller way this contrast can be grasped by comparing two fragmentary ornaments of Queen Nofretari (Fig. 96) with the Middle Kingdom electrum uraeus in Fig. 66. The former seem to have come from the tomb of the wife of Ram-

145

96. Jewelry of Queen Nofretari

esses II which is so justly famous for its lovely paintings. The placques are simi-lar, although of different size. The smaller is gold, while the other is of silver covered with gold leaf. Both are inlaid with lapis lazuli, carnelian, and beryl. On the smaller one, which is an element from a bracelet, the name and titles of No-fretari are embossed in the gold and flanked by a border of inlaid feather pattern. The other, which comes from an unidentified piece of jewelry, has a similar bor-der enclosing the titles of the queen, with the hieroglyphs made up of inlaid stones.

One of the most developed crafts of the Ramesside period was the making of brilliantly colored glazed tiles for use in wall decoration. These have been found in great numbers, both in the Delta palaces of the kings Ramesses II and Rames-ses III and in the latter's palace attached to the temple of Medinet Habu at Thebes. It is from the last named place that the finest of our tiles come, although some of the smaller pieces were found at Tell el Yahudiyeh in the Delta. These flat pieces with figures moulded in relief were used in designs framing doorways, or in panels along the base of the wall. Sometimes they were combined with quite large pieces of sculpture in the round, executed in the same glazed technique, to ornament the steps of the king's throne.

The employment of glazed tiles for architectural decoration goes back to a very early period, and was used with striking effect in the blue walls, imitating mat-work, of the chambers under the Step Pyramid in the time of Zoser. It was peculiarly favored by the Egyptian colony at Kerma in the Middle Kingdom, where the craftsmen attempted quite large pieces in the round and inlay pieces like the lions and head of a prisoner in our collection, which are not unlike the Ramesside work in spirit. However, at no other time did the craftsmen achieve such rich effects of coloring as they did in the tiles representing foreign captives from Medinet Habu (Fig. 97). Here also is a fascinating delineation of the different types of foreign peoples who at this time menaced Egypt's security. The negroes in their gay costumes are familiar to us from numerous sources in the paintings and reliefs of the time. The Hittite, Philistine, and two types of Syrians all wear similar long robes covered with gaudy embroidery. But the beardless Hittite has been given a snub-nosed brutal face, the red-skinned Philistine wears a high feathered headdress, while the Amorite is differentiated from the bearded, black-haired Syrian by his shaven head. Prof. Hölscher's reconstructed drawing shows such a tile revetment in the doorway opening from the palace onto the ' balcony of appearances ' in the first court of the temple of Medinet Habu. An

97. Wall tiles: Syrians, Philistine and Negro

actual inlaid door-frame was also found in the debris of the palace. The decoration of these doors included not only the tiles of foreigners and small figures of *rekhyt*-birds with upraised human hands which represent the people of Egypt bowing before Pharaoh but figures of the king as well. Our red glass face of Ramesses III (which has now turned green with age) was combined with other glass inlays and faience wig-pieces to form a group showing the king with one of the ladies of his household (Fig. 98). This evidently came from the architrave of a stone door-frame in the mud-brick palace that adjoins the first court of the Medinet Habu temple in Western Thebes. It resembles the informal representations of the king with harîm ladies which are carved in relief on the stone walls of the pavillion over the gateway to this temple.

98. Glass and faience inlays of Ramesses III and a court lady

Chapter V

Egypt in the Late Period

THE HISTORICAL BACKGROUND: DYNASTIES XXI–XXV

THE TALE of Wenamon clearly illustrates the decline that had set in by the end of Ramesside times. Although Ramesses XI was on the throne, it was the High Priest of Amon, Herihor, who sent Wenamon to Syria to fetch timber for the Divine Bark of the god. Also his commission had to be approved by Smendes and his wife Tentamon, who were ' the rulers whom Amon hath given to the north of his land,' as Wenamon himself describes them to Zakar-baal of Byblos. Not only was Egypt's rule divided at home but little respect was left for her abroad, as the misfortunes of Amon's representative show only too vividly. Robbed at Dor and insulted by the king of Byblos, Wenamon, when he finally obtained the timber, was set upon by pirates and driven ashore by a storm on the coast of Cyprus. There he narrowly escaped death at the hands of the natives. Ample payment was expected for the Lebanon cedar, which in the time of Egypt's might would have been exacted as tribute.

At the death of Herihor, Smendes seems to have controlled the whole country for a while. He was succeeded on the throne of Tanis by Pasebkhanu I, who in turn was followed by his son-in-law, the Theban priest Paynozem. From this fact we can see that the High Priests of Amon at Thebes were in close relationship with the Tanite Dynasty. While controlling the southern part of the country, they do not seem to have been on hostile terms with the northern kings. Very little is known about the last three Tanite kings, Amen-em-ipet, Sa-amon, and Pasebkhanu II. The succession of the priest-kings at Thebes has been reconstructed from the wrappings of the mummies in the Deir el Bahari cache, where these men were buried beside the bodies of the great kings of the New Kingdom, which had been collected here for protection against the incessant tomb robberies that had grown acute in the reign of Ramesses IX. The last of the burials in this cache were made under Sheshonq I. The intact burial of Pasebkhanu I, the first of the northern kings of Dynasty XXI, has recently been discovered in a tomb within the precinct of the temple at Tanis. In neighboring chambers was found the similarly magnificent equipment deposited with the silver coffin of an as yet unidentified king Sheshonq, as well as the disturbed burials of Osorkon II and Takelot II of Dynasty XXII. Thus the temple of Tanis had replaced the Valley of the Kings at Thebes as the burial ground of the Pharaohs of this time.

From the genealogy of a certain Harpeson, inscribed upon a stela set up in the Serapeum at Saqqarah late in Dynasty XXII, we learn that the family of kings who succeeded Pasebkhanu II was of Libyan origin. The dynasty is usually termed Bubastite, although its kings were buried at Tanis and had originally come from Heracleopolis. Toward the end of Dynasty XX, or shortly afterwards, the Libyan Buyuwawa settled at Heracleopolis where his son became chief priest of the Temple of Harsaphes, a post which was to remain in the control of the family for many generations. Some years later, a descendant of Buyuwawa, the Great Chief Sheshonq, wished to establish a funerary cult for his father, Nemrat, at Abydos, and demanded that his inheritance of Nemrat's offices be confirmed by the king. This request was submitted to an oracle of Amon, a procedure that was often followed at this time. In this incident one can feel the growing power of the Heracleopolitan princes, and it is likely that the ruler (probably Pasebkhanu II) did not feel strong enough to issue judgments without cloaking them with the authority of Amon. Not long after this Nemrat's son seized the Tanite throne, undoubtedly with the help of the Libyan mercenaries which he, like his predecessors, commanded as Great Chief of the Ma (a shortened form of the Mesh-wesh Libyans). Sheshonq I soon gained control of the whole country, and his strong administration was able to check Egypt's decline by restoring a considerable measure of prosperity at home and the country's prestige abroad.

Throughout the troubled years that had followed Ramesside times, the thoroughly Egyptianized country of Kush (Ethiopia) to the south had remained loyal to Thebes. The religious ties were particularly close between the priesthood of Amon at Thebes and that of Amon, Lord of the Holy Mountain, at Napata. The Asiatic empire in Palestine and Syria had, on the other hand, broken entirely away from its masters, and we have seen how little respect the ruler of Byblos had entertained for an Egyptian envoy in the time of Herihor. Palestine had as yet nothing to fear from Assyria's growing power and the kingdom of Israel had been consolidated by David and Solomon, who amassed great wealth in Jerusalem. Egypt had maintained peaceful relations with Solomon, who even took an Egyptian princess in marriage. But in the fifth year of the reign of Solomon's successor, Sheshonq attacked Palestine. This expedition was probably little more than a raid, and it is possible that the strongly fortified city of Jerusalem was not really captured and sacked, but that Rehoboam bought his city's immunity with the treasure from the Temple and Solomon's palace. While Egypt did not attempt to hold Palestine, she regained something of her former influence and profited by a greatly increased foreign trade. That it was foolish to depend upon her support was to be proved many times. She could do little to assist the coalition that unsuccessfully opposed Shalmaneser III in 853 B.C. at Qarqar, and it was probably Takelot II who sent a present of camels and a hippopotamus, along with the tribute of Israel, Tyre, and Sidon to the Assyrian king while he was having his triumphal stela carved at the Nahr-el-Kelb in 841 B.C.

The dynasty founded by Sheshonq lasted for about two hundred years, but toward the end of that time Egypt was hopelessly divided into squabbling little kingdoms and menaced both by Assyria and a powerful, independent Kush. Sheshonq was followed by a series of kings alternately bearing the names of Osorkon, Takelot, and Sheshonq. The family followed the policy, instituted in Dynasty XXI, of establishing the son of the reigning king as High Priest of Thebes, but the High Priesthood of Harsaphes at Heracleopolis also remained an important family perquisite. In the reign of Takelot II a civil war broke out in which the High Priest Osorkon was forced to fly from Thebes. At the end of some fifteen years of dissension, a man named Pedibast succeeded in setting up a rival dynasty in 817 B.C., which ran parallel with Dynasty XXII until the Ethiopian conquest, about 730 B.C. Although Manetho calls this new twenty-third dynasty Tanite, the kings continued to bear the names of Sheshonq, Osorkon, and Takelot, and seem to be closely related to the Bubastite house. The confusion which resulted from this divided power enabled a number of local dynasts to set themselves up in northern Egypt. Osorkon III of Dynasty XXIII established his daughter Shepenwepet as Priestess of Amon in Thebes, and the Kushite kings made further use of this evident attempt to break the temporal power of the Priesthood of Amon. After the conquest, a female line of High Priestesses was instituted when Piankhy forced Shepenwepet to adopt as her successor Amenirdis, the daughter of his predecessor Kashta.

The origin of the independent kingdom of Kush is still somewhat obscure. At El Kurru, in the Sudan, the Museum's Expedition found the burial places of several generations of the chiefs who preceded Kashta and Piankhy, and it is possible to see the growth of their power in the increasing size of their tombs. Dr. Reisner believed that the family which was to form Dynasty XXV after the conquest of Egypt was of Libyan origin, representing an infiltration into the Sudan similar to that which had brought the ancestors of Sheshonq as settlers to Heracleopolis. Certainly Piankhy, the first member of the family about whom we have any precise information, seems thoroughly Egyptian. To be reckoned with as a civilizing influence was the power of the Egyptian priests of the Temple of Amon at Gebel Barkal near Napata, the capital of the new kings. The Kushite kings were to show themselves as piously disposed toward Amon as any Theban. Possibly Piankhy owed his claim to the Egyptian throne to a relationship with a General Pashedenbast, whose name was found inscribed upon an alabaster vessel at the Nuri pyramids. Pashedenbast is known from a Karnak inscription to have been the son of a King Sheshonq who was a contemporary of Pedibast, probably Sheshonq III.

Piankhy's invasion of Egypt was instigated by the appearance of a new power in the Delta. Tef-nekht of Sais had succeeded in uniting the dynasts of Lower Egypt, presumably having disposed of the last Sheshonq of Dynasty XXII. He had occupied Memphis and was laying siege to Heracleopolis. When Piankhy learned that the ruler of Hermopolis in Middle Egypt had joined forces with Tef-nekht, he sent an army into Egypt. The Kushites met Tef-nekht's forces ascending the Nile and defeated them in a battle on the river. Tef-nekht escaped to the Delta, while Nemrat of Hermopolis managed to return to the defense of his city. Piankhy, disturbed by this ambiguous victory, decided to conduct the campaign in person. He proceeded to Thebes, where he took part in the great feast of Opet and then hurried northwards to besiege Hermopolis. The Kushite forces proved too strong for Nemrat, who was only able to obtain terms by sending out his wife to intercede for him. We learn from Piankhy's triumphal stela that he was furious at the treatment of Nemrat's horses, which had been starved during the siege. Piankhy's love of horses is also attested by the fact that his favorite steeds were buried near his pyramid at El Kurru, a custom which was followed by his successors.

Relieving Tef-nekht's siege of Heracleopolis, the Kushite army proceeded to the attack of Memphis, which was taken by the ingenious use of boats brought up to the side of the city exposed to a high Nile flood. With the fall of Memphis all the powers of the Delta submitted to Piankhy, including a King Osorkon, probably the last of the line of Dynasty XXIII, who had previously fled from Thebes. Tef-nekht himself escaped into the impenetrable swamps of the Delta. Any attempt to capture him would have proved too costly and his nominal submission was accepted. Instead of remaining to consolidated his gains, Piankhy returned almost immediately to Napata, leaving the Delta to break forth into prompt revolt. Tef-nekht returned, regaining the northern country as far as Memphis. Piankhy made no further attempt to interfere in the Delta. It was probably Tef-nekht who made a treaty with Hoshea of Samaria against the Assyrians, although he can have given little aid to the king of Israel when his city was besieged by Shalmaneser V and finally captured by Sargon II. The Assyrian advance into Palestine must have been very alarming to the people of the Delta, and Tef-nekht's successor, Bakenrenef, whom the Greeks called Bocchoris and Manetho lists as the single king of Dynasty XXIV, gave what support he could to the resistance against Sargon's army. His general was disastrously beaten at Raphia in 720 B.C., and we find the Egyptian king attempting to placate Sargon with tribute in 715. Tef-nekht and Bakenrenef were the earliest of the Egyptian kings known to the Greeks, and it has been thought that the rise of Sais was due to the growing commerce with the sea-faring Ionian traders, who may already have founded the Milesian trading station near the Canopic mouth of the Nile, which was later to become the important town of Naukratis. Bocchoris, according to Greek tradition, was a wealthy prince who was renowned as a law-giver. His reign was brought sharply to an end about 715 B.C. by Shabako, who invaded Egypt soon after his succession to the throne. According to Manetho he captured Bocchoris and burned him alive.

Shabako continued the ineffectual resistance to the Assyrians, and in 700 B.C. his army supporting Sidon and Hezekiah of Judah was badly defeated by Sennacherib, with the resultant capture of Lachish so vividly illustrated by the reliefs of the Assyrian king in the British Museum. Hezekiah must ruefully have considered Egyptian support a ' bruised reed.' That Shabako made some sort of terms with Assyria is suggested by a clay sealing with his name found in Sennacherib's palace at Nineveh. Shabako was succeeded by Shebitku, about whose reign little is known, and he in turn was succeeded by Taharqa. Taharqa's encounter with Sennacherib at Pelusium, with the ensuing miracle of the mice which ate the strings of the Assyrian's bows, as recounted by Herodotus, or the decimation of Sennacherib's forces, as in the Biblical account, seems to lack confirmation. It may be confused with a later attempt at invasion by Esarhaddon which is supposed to have been turned back by a storm. It is not impossible, however, that Taharqa may have served in Palestine as general under Shebitku in support of Jerusalem, and that the Assyrian army was afflicted by a plague which forced its retreat.

Taharqa had gone north as a young man of twenty, perhaps accompanying Shabako in his conquest of the Delta. When his mother came north to see him after his coronation, it is particularly remarked that she had not seen him since he left Napata many years before. Taharqa made his capital at Tanis, evidently with the idea that he could keep a better watch on the movements of the Assyrians from there. His apprehensions were justified. Esarhaddon had determined that Egypt must be crushed, for while she maintained hardly more than a sphere of influence in Palestine, even the illusion of her former power was sufficient to stir up rebellion in Syria and Palestine against Assyria. The invasion of 675 B.C. was halted by a great storm, which may have been the origin of the legends concerning the catastrophe which overtook Sennacherib's army. However, in 671, Esarhaddon made a swift and easy conquest of the country, defeating Taharqa, who fled to Napata, and capturing Memphis and the family of the Ethiopian king. All of the petty rulers submitted to Esarhaddon as far up the river as Thebes. Of these, the most important were the governor of Thebes, who had a long career, and Necho, the prince of Sais, who was especially favored by the Assyrians and whose son was eventually able to gain his independence and establish Dynasty XXVI. Esarhaddon rather overestimated his conquest when he showed the king of Tyre and Taharqa as captives on his triumphal stela at Senjirli. The besieged city of Tyre was still rejecting the Assyrian terms for surrender, while Taharqa had safely reached Napata.

When he heard of the death of Esarhaddon, Taharqa reoccupied Egypt, but was driven out again in 667 B.C. by Ashurbanipal. In the next year a revolt in the Delta broke out, but the Assyrians dealt leniently with Necho. He was replaced at Sais, and his son was made governor of Athribis. Again in 663 Taharqa's successor, Tanwetamani, invaded Egypt and laid siege to Memphis. He was easily defeated by Ashurbanipal, who this time followed the retreating Kushites into Upper Egypt and sacked Thebes. The sack of Thebes made a terrible impression upon the ancient world, as can be seen from the well-known words of the Prophet Nahum, who forecast similar destruction for Nineveh. Actually Mentuemhat, its governor, survived the spoiling of the city and returned to make some restorations in its temples. He participated in the ceremonies when Nitocris, the daughter of Psamtik I, came south to be adopted as High Priestess of Amon by Piankhy's daughter Shepenwepet II. Because of the vivid portraiture of his statues in the Cairo Museum and the fact that we know his tomb at Thebes, Mentuemhat stands out more clearly as a personality than do most of the other figures who participated in the catastrophe of Thebes. The city never recovered from the blow. The successors of Tanwetamani remained at Napata and made no further attempts to regain Egypt, while the Saite Dynasty, which soon threw off the Assyrian yoke, chose to keep the seat of their power in Lower Egypt. The loss of Thebes' prominence was probably due less to the harm done by the Assyrians than to the fact that the Kushites had broken the power of the Priesthood of Amon by setting up the female line of priestesses. Thus Psamtik and his followers were no longer faced with the problem of a rival power in Upper Egypt, a factor which had contributed largely to the weakness of the royal house in the time before Piankhy.

THE SAITE AND PTOLEMAIC PERIODS: DYNASTIES XXVI–XXXI

ASHURBANIPAL'S WITHDRAWAL to Nineveh after the sack of Thebes left Psamtik, the son of Necho, in a very strong position in the Delta. The Assyrians could no longer turn their attention to Egypt. The Scythians were pushing the Cimmerian tribes against the northern borders of the Assyrian Empire, while civil war between Nineveh and Babylon occupied Ashurbanipal at home. His last years were darkened by illness and family strife. The forty-three years of Ashurbanipal's reign had seemed a kind of Golden Age but they were to be followed by rapid dissolution, the destruction of Nineveh, and the scattering of the Assyrian people. The Saite Dynasty was to witness not only the fall of Nineveh, but the collapse of the short-lived Babylonian Empire with the capture of Babylon by Cyrus, and the subsequent conquest of Egypt by the Persians. Within the space of a hundred years the three great capitals of the ancient world were overrun by an invader, Thebes in 663 B.C., Nineveh in 612, and Babylon in 539, fulfilling in a terrifying way the warnings of the Hebrew Prophet.

Psamtik had gradually assumed independent power and in 658 B.C., with the help of Gyges of Lydia, he was able to throw off at last all vestiges of Assyrian overlordship. It was probably the assistance of Ionian and Carian mercenaries that gave rise to Herodotus' story of the brazen men who came to Psamtik's help in answer to an oracle of Buto. Egypt's independence was not a great loss to Assyria since friendly relations were maintained and Psamtik's successor Necho gave what assistance he could to the Assyrians against the Babylonians. Although he did not yet control Upper Egypt, Psamtik negotiated the adoption of his daughter Nitocris by the High Priestess of Amon. By placing one of his own men in Edfu and extending the powers of the Nomarch of Heracleopolis, the Saite king was able to limit the power of Mentuemhat, the Prince of Thebes, both in Upper Egypt and at Thebes itself. He also replaced the Libyans in his army by Greek mercenaries, and by encouraging the Greek merchants built up a thriving foreign trade. These Greek traders and soldiers clashed more than once with the local inhabitants, and by the time of Amasis anti-foreign feeling had grown so strong that the garrisons had to be withdrawn from the frontier fortress of Daphnae to Memphis, and the Greek traders confined to the treaty port of Naukratis.

Necho, Psamtik's successor, was able to regain a large part of Palestine and Egypt, as a result of the destruction of the Assyrian power by Nabopolassar of Babylon and the Medes under Cyaxares. He was less successful when he attempted to help the remnant of the Assyrian armies against Nebuchadnezzar, the son of the Babylonian king. Necho was ignominiously defeated at Carchemish and forced to abandon his gains in Palestine. The Saite kings were never able to regain possession of the country inland. Apries with his fleet managed to dominate the coastal regions of Syria and Palestine, although he could do nothing to prevent the capture of Jerusalem by Nebuchadnezzar. His successor, Amasis, continued to control the coast and also captured Cyprus. Apries had been strongly under the control of the Greek faction in the Delta, and when Amasis seized the throne with the aid of disaffected soldiery he was forced to adopt an anti-Greek policy, which he gradually relinquished as soon as he felt more sure of himself. The end of his reign was clouded by the danger of the rising Persian power. Cyrus overthrew the Medes in 550 B.C. Croesus of Lydia, after trying to get help from Egypt, was defeated in 546, while Babylon fell in 539. Amasis was spared the fate of Croesus. He died in 526, leaving Psamtik III to face the Persian conquest under Cambyses, an invasion which had perhaps not been contemplated by Cyrus.

With the occupation of the country by the soldiers of Cambyses the history of Egypt as an independent power is practically ended. Manetho indeed lists five more dynasties, but of these Dynasties XXVII and XXXI consisted of the kings of Persia, while Dynasty XXVIII was the rule of a local dynast, Amyrtaios, who organized a revolt during the troubled reign of Darius II. By means of alliances with Athens and Sparta the kings of Dynasties XXIX and XXX were able to maintain the independence thus gained for about sixty years. The two kings Nectanebo I and II of Dynasty XXX are the best known of these rulers, because of their numerous monuments. Teos, the son of Nectanebo I, was almost successful in regaining a part of Egypt's empire in Asia with the help of the Greeks. The treachery of his brother, who was supported by the Spartan general, rendered these early gains ephemeral, however. Teos fled to the Persians, while Nectanebo II seized the Egyptian throne. With the advent of Artaxerxes III to the throne of Persia, a determined effort to regain control of Egypt resulted in the defeat of Nectanebo. Thus the second Persian domination began in 341 B.C. This was soon brought to an end by Alexander, who invaded Egypt in 332 after crushing the Persians in the battle of Issus.

When Alexander the Great died of a fever in Nebuchadnezzar's palace in Babylon in 323, his great empire was divided up amongst his Macedonian generals. Ptolemy, the son of Lagos, was appointed Satrap of Egypt by the new Macedonian king, the feeble half-brother of Alexander, Philip Arrhidaeus. Plans were made to bury Alexander in the temple of Amon in the Oasis of Siwa, but Ptolemy determined to make political capital of the possession of the body and deflected the funeral cortege to Memphis. After remaining some time in Memphis the burial was transferred to a tomb erected at Alexandria, the city founded by the Macedonian conqueror which was to become the capital of the Ptolemies.

Ptolemy at first maintained a nominal allegiance to the Macedonian House. Such monuments as the shrine at Karnak were inscribed in the name of Philip Arrhidaeus. But on learning of the murder of that young man and the subsequent death of the child Alexander, Ptolemy felt free to declare himself king of Egypt. By the end of his reign he also held Palestine, Cyprus, Cyrenaica, and a Protectorate over the Cyclades. His power in Egypt rested upon a ruling class of Greeks and upon military colonists who had been attracted to Egypt and were now settled at strategic points throughout the country. One farsighted move was the institution of the official worship of Serapis which had an appeal for both Greeks and Egyptians. This god united the properties of Osiris and Apis, as well as being a form of the Greek Zeus.

The luxury-loving Philadelphus was a contrast to his warrior father. Although his reign saw the first Syrian war and a struggle with Macedon for control of the sea, the interests of the second Ptolemy were directed chiefly toward the arts and sciences. His generous patronage drew a brilliant group of men to Egypt, and the fame of the Alexandrine Museum rapidly increased. The government was really in large part in the hands of Arsinoe II who soon replaced the first wife of Philadelphus. Arsinoe was one of those able and ruthless women of the Macedonian royal house, whose energy from time to time served as a balance to the indolence and lethargy of the male Ptolemies. The banishment of her predecessor Arsinoe I, who was actually her own step-daughter, anticipates the complicated family relationships and callous cruelty that grew ever more hideous in the midst of the luxurious opulence of the Ptolemaic court.

The third Ptolemy, Euergetes, was tempted into a military expedition by the quarreling Seleucid family which resulted in a truly brilliant feat. The king apparently penetrated as far as Persia and was reputed to have brought back from there the statues which had been carried off from Egypt. Ptolemy then rested on his laurels for twenty years, during which Egypt remained prosperous and the activities of the Alexandrine Museum went on undiminished. However, Euergetes' successor Ptolemy IV, Philopator, brought Egypt to a feeble condition from which she never rose again. A literary and aesthetic voluptuary whose mind was occupied by such projects as the building of his famous pleasure ship on the Nile, Philopator left the governing of the country to a cunning old scoundrel named Sosibius. The queen, Arsinoe III, disgusted by the extravagances of her husband over whom she had no control, remained shut up within her apartments in the palace. Sosibius surprised the world by defeating the Seleucid king Antiochus at Raphia, but this triumph was to have a peculiar repercussion at home. Part of the success had been due to the native levies of troops which had fought for the first time beside Greek soldiers. The result was a tremendous surge of nationalistic feeling in Egypt. The building of temples to the old gods had by no means satisfied native aspirations, and an uprising broke out which was not completely suppressed for a long time. The construction of the temple of Edfu had to be stopped for twenty years, and at one time the building was occupied by the insurgents.

The murder of Arsinoe at the death of Ptolemy IV and the announcement of the infant Epiphanes as Ptolemy V caused a furious outbreak in Alexandria which overwhelmed Sosibius. Macedon and Seleucia fell upon Egypt's possessions abroad. A succession of regents followed Sosibius. The boy king was crowned in Memphis in an attempt to gain native support, while the decree on the Rosetta stone represents a conciliatory gesture to the priesthood. Epiphanes reigned for over twenty years, during which Egypt watched with alarm the contest between Antiochus of Syria and the formidable power of Rome, which now reached out into the east to smash this old rival of the Ptolemies. Antiochus IV, who invaded Egypt after the accession of Ptolemy VI, Philometor, was forced to withdraw merely by the weight of a Roman embassy. Philometor had fled to Rome when Euergetes II was placed on the throne by the revolting Alexandrians, but he returned to Egypt backed by Roman support. Having once suffered the shameful insult of Antiochus playing Pharaoh in Memphis, a strange turn in fortune came for Philometor when, interceding in the affairs of the Seleucid Kingdom, he was offered the crown in Antioch. He was soon afterwards killed by being thrown from his horse in battle. Euergetes promptly seized the Egyptian throne again, married Cleopatra II, the wife of Philometor, and murdered the young Ptolemy who was the rightful heir to the throne.

Euergetes II was enormously fat and is described contemptuously by Scipio Aemilianus as being hardly able to walk in a state procession from the ships, when he received the Roman embassy that had come to examine the situation in Egypt. Revolt was seething in Alexandria and the following dynastic struggles, in which one ineffectual Ptolemy replaced another, were overshadowed by the growing menace of Rome. The final result is familiar to all. Caesar, pursuing Pompey to Egypt, supported Cleopatra VII against her brother. For a time it seemed as though this fascinating woman might restore Egypt's waning strength, first by her influence over Caesar and then, even after his assassination, by the charms which she exerted upon Antony. But the battle of Actium sealed Antony's doom and Cleopatra, realizing that she could do nothing with the young Octavian, killed herself. Octavian put to death the boy Caesarion whom Cleopatra had borne to Caesar, and with him the rule of the Ptolemies came to an end in 30 B.C. From the time of Augustus, Egypt was treated as a Roman province and its further history as a part of the empire need hardly concern us here, except for certain contacts between the emissaries of Caesar and the still independent Ethiopian land in the south.

To go back several hundred years, Tanwetamani, when he was driven out of Egypt by the Assyrians in 663 B.C., retired, depleted of manpower and resources, to his kingdom in the south. However, the gold mines and the trade routes of that country remained capable of making Ethiopia (Kush) prosperous again. Tanwetamani was succeeded by a series of strong rulers who maintained their capital at Napata, and who continued to be buried with their ancestors at the pyramid sites of El Kurru and Nuri. Of the descendants of Taharqa the most important were the four kings, Atlanersa, Senkamanisken, Anlamani, and Aspelta, who ruled in that order. There were two other lesser kings of the Second Dynasty, and these were followed by a series of kings who claimed descent from Taharqa. All but one of these were buried at Nuri, like their predecessors. This man built his tomb beside that of Piankhy at El Kurru, the old cemetery of the founders of the Kingdom. Although until the time of Nastasen (337 B.C.) the kings continued to be buried in the royal cemetery at Nuri, the seat of government had been transferred to Meroë in the latter part of the sixth century. Thus, first from Napata and later from Meroë for about three hundred and fifty years, from the beginning of the Saite period until well along in the reign of the first Ptolemy, the successors of Kashta and Piankhy maintained an undivided rule over the country from the district just south of Aswan to the region around Khartum.

The influence of Egyptian culture became gradually weaker, fostered only by the contacts of merchants, the occasional importation of craftsmen, and possibly by visits of the priests to Egyptian temples. Cut off politically from the northern land which they had once ruled, the Kushite kings were turning to the development of the country to the south of them. We can see the effects of this southern contact even before the shift of the capital from the old cultural center of Napata to Meroë. Although about 300 B.C. a few kings seem to have ruled independently at Napata, the preponderance of influence was to remain in the south with the kings who had established themselves at Meroë. A flourishing period set in with the advent of Ergamenes to the Meroitic throne about 248 B.C. Diodorus tells us that this king received a Greek education during the reign of Ptolemy II. Certainly he employed good sculptors from Egypt to decorate the temple which he built at Dakka in Lower Nubia. Ptolemy IV added to this building, while Ergamenes executed some work on another structure commenced by Ptolemy IV at Philae. If a statue from Gebel Barkal is to be identified as Ergamenes, an Egyptian sculptor must also have traveled to Napata in his reign. No imported Hellenistic objects were found in the tomb of Ergamenes or in those of his immediate successors, although a few pieces of silver (Fig. 124, Nos. 27.874, 24.1041) had been placed in tombs of the late fourth and early third centuries B.C. Early contact between Meroë and the Greek world is indicated by the discovery of the Amazon Rhyton (Fig. 120). It was signed by the Athenian Sotades who worked

99. Gold figurine of the god Harsaphes. Dyn. XXV

in the middle of the fifth century B.C. However, the evidence from the Meroë cemetery suggests that the chief period for the importation of Alexandrian and Roman bronzes and silver was in the first and second centuries A.D.

The flowering of Meroitic culture in the period between 248 B.C. and A.D. 25 was temporarily interrupted when in 23 B.C. a Roman expedition under Petronius attacked Napata and destroyed it. It seems to have been Queen Amanishakhete of Meroë who brought about the country's recovery. It was possibly this queen who, two years after Petronius retired from Napata, sent an embassy to Augustus who was then at Samos. The accident that there should be a ruling queen-regent at Meroë at the time of Petronius' invasion, probably gave an added advantage to the Romans and at the same time may have been the origin of their belief that Ethiopia was ruled by a series of queens, or Candaces. In the last phase of Meroitic culture some twenty-one kings and queens ruled with declining power, threatened by the rise of Abyssinian Axum. As she grew weaker, Meroë was less able to control the unruly desert tribes that threatened the trade routes in the region of the Nile cataracts and which were a source of constant annoyance to the Roman governors of Egypt. As early as the reign of Nero envoys were sent to Ethiopia, ostensibly to explore the sources of the Nile. These men brought back such a dreary account of the impoverished and thinly populated land that Rome showed little further interest in the country beyond the border tribes who molested the Aswan frontier.

The reliefs of the pyramid chapels at Begarawiyeh, the cemetery of Meroë, and at Gebel Barkal, where were buried the rulers of independent Napata, show the gradual increase in native African elements in the art of the Meroitic Kingdoms. The enormously fat figures and negroid faces of these people, in their embroidered and tasselled robes, retain little that reminds one of Egypt. Up until the time of Ergamenes the use of Egyptian hieroglyphics had been maintained, but in the group of tombs which follow that king's pyramid at Begarawiyeh the hieroglyphic inscriptions become faltering and disappear altogether. Egyptian is the subject matter of the funerary rites represented on the walls, with illustrations taken from the Book of the Dead, but the execution of these scenes was drawing farther and farther away from its sources. The crowded compositions, with their confused pattern of little figures in high, rounded relief, reach their most characteristic stage in the chapels that follow closely on the period of Ergamenes. The most developed example of the native style is to be seen in the chapel of Queen Amanishakhete and in the early decorations with which Natakamani adorned the Lion Temple at Naga, where we find the use of Meroitic hieroglyphic writing. These decorations have a barbaric strength, as in the huge, bulky figures of Queen Amanishakhete striking down captives, in the old pharaonic tradition, on the chapel pylon. Perhaps these scenes actually refer to the country's struggles under that queen. After the earliest work on the Naga temple, Natakamani imported an Egyptian scribe, possibly for the redecoration of the Barkal temple made necessary by the destruction of Petronius. Correct hieroglyphic inscriptions begin to appear at Napata, as well as in the chapel of the crown prince and that of his mother. In the later constructions of Natakamani, while the king's name is in Egyptian hieroglyphics, the other inscriptions are in Meroitic. From then on the use of Meroitic becomes preponderant, and we find, during the last decline before the invasion of Axum, that native African elements accompany a steady degeneration of craftsmanship.

Thus, with the gradual disappearance of Egyptian influence in the Sudan, we come to the end. The Ethiopians had been slow to forget, as Dr. Reisner has said, but little that was creative or constructive had been added to the dying forms. In Egypt itself the Egyptian style dragged itself out under the later Roman Empire and at the beginning of Byzantine rule. But any stimulating forces in the culture of the Nile Valley now came from the impetus of growing Christianity and were foreign to what had gone before. With the closing of the pagan temples by Justinian in 543 A.D., ancient Egyptian civilization came to an end.

OBJECTS OF THE LATE PERIOD

CHARACTERISTIC of Dynasty XXI is the brilliant blue glaze used on small objects from the burials of the families of the High Priests of Amon in the Deir el Bahari Cache. Such are the little shawabti figures which were intended to take the place of their owners for any work that they might be called upon to do in the Underworld. We have examples of Queen Maat-ka-ra (Nos. 56.1269, 57.407, 408) and Queen Henet-tawy (No. 56.314), the wives of Paynozem I. Other important persons of the period are represented by the shawabtis loaned to us by Horace L. Mayer: Paynozem himself, his daughter, Iset-m-kheb, the owner of the decorated leather funeral tent in Cairo, and Masaharta who succeeded his father Paynozem as High Priest. Two blue glazed faience cups belonged to the Princess Nesi-khonsu (Nos. 97.901, 56.313), the wife of the High Priest Paynozem II, and a faience pectoral (No. 56.315) which probably also came from the Deir el Bahari Cache. The daughter of Iset-m-kheb and the High Priest Menkheperra, who was named Henet-tawy after her grandmother, was buried in a set of wooden coffins found at Thebes by the expedition of the Metropolitan Museum (Nos. 56.639, 640). A detail of the fine painted plaster reliefs on the outer coffin shows the princess making an offering before a recumbent figure of Osiris (Fig. 100).

The brightly painted cartonnage mummy cases of a somewhat later time (Dynasties XXII to XXV; Nos. 72.4832, 33, 37) do not show such superlative workmanship as those of the families of the High Priests of Amon. They represent the mummy in its form as Osiris and are covered with ritualistic scenes and inscriptions. Their type changed little as time went on and these resemble the well preserved coffins containing the mummy of Nes-mut-aat-neru (No. 95.1407) of Dynasty XXVI from Deir el Bahari. The linen wrapped body of the latter is covered with a bead net and was placed in an inner and outer case. A more elaborately fashioned net is that found in one of the early graves of the Ethiopian

100. Princess Henet-tawy offering to Osiris. Dyn. XXI

period at Meroë. The original stringing was carefully noted and restored by Mrs. Reisner (No. 27.443). The design contains a human face surmounting a winged scarab, a figure of Isis with outspread wings, and the four genii of the dead followed by funerary inscriptions. Similar in technique are the two bags made of colored beads (Nos. 24.648, 649), also of the Ethiopian period from Meroë. The bead mummy nets were evidently a cheaper imitation of the expensive trappings of an earlier princess of the sixth century B.C. (No. 23.1396) where a finely worked mask, collar, winged scarab and other parts were made of silver.

With the Deir el Bahari mummy mentioned above were found two boxes containing the shawabtis of that lady. The lids of the two boxes are painted with representations of the funerary bark. An important part of the equipment of these late burials was the papyrus covered with magic texts and pictures to protect the dead person in his journey through the Underworld. A good example of such a Book of the Dead is the papyrus of the Singer in the Temple of Amon, Ta-amon (Fig. 101), which has each Chapter illustrated by the proper vignettes. At the right, in the largest picture, appears the Judgment of the Dead before Osiris. The dead woman is ushered forward by the Goddess of Truth, while Horus and Anubis weigh the heart of Ta-amon against the Feather of Truth on the scales. Thoth stands ready to record the decision, with the monster Amemet crouching before him ready to gobble up the soul if it be found wanting. The Museum's

163

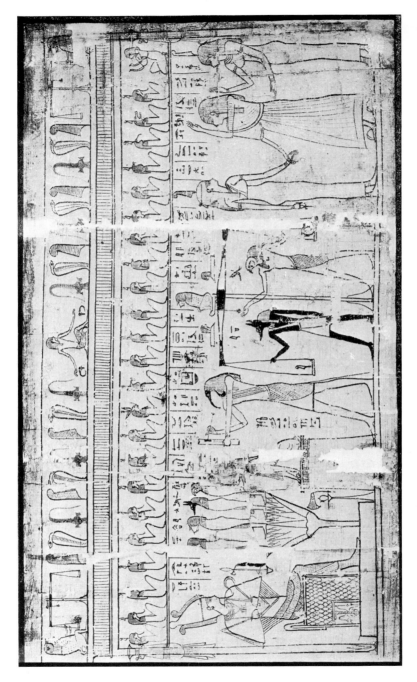

101. Judgment scene. Papyrus of Ta-amon

collection is rich in the numerous scarabs and amulets which, when placed upon the mummy, were supposed to add further protection to the dead man against the actively evil spirits which peopled the Underworld.

Very important, both as a work of art and as an historical document, is the tiny, beautifully-worked gold statuette of the ram-god Harsaphes (Fig. 99). It was found at Heracleopolis by Sir Flinders Petrie and is inscribed with the name of the local dynast who resisted the Delta coalition of Tef-nekht at the time when Piankhy decided to invade Egypt. This masterpiece of the goldsmith's art, which is fine enough to stand beside many an earlier work, brings us to the Kushite Dynasty XXV. The Museum possesses an outstanding collection of material excavated in the tombs of the Kushite kings at the pyramids of El Kurru and Nuri, and in the temple of Amon at Gebel Barkal (Fig. 102). Of the larger pieces of sculpture which decorated that temple, we have no examples of the time when the Kushites were ruling Egypt. We possess, however, an important series of monuments erected at Gebel Barkal by the kings who immediately succeeded the rout of Tanwetamani by the Assyrians. These follow closely the style of Dynasty XXV in Egypt.

The colossal statue of Anlamani (No. 23.732), that of Aspelta (Fig. 103) which is nearly as large, and the smaller figure of Senkamanisken (No. 23.731), conform to the type set by the realistically modelled head of Taharqa in the Cairo Museum, and to other sculpture which was found at Thebes. The head is small for the body, the skull rounded and high for its narrow depth from front to back. Such a skull formation is found in Kushite statues and reliefs of the early period and appears again in the reliefs of Psamtik I and Nectanebo I in the British Museum. Our statues have heavy features with a broad flat nose and full lips. The same brutal realism is even more marked in the nearly contemporaneous Cairo statues of Mentuemhat, the Governor of Thebes. Two more or less incompatible strains entered into the art of Dynasty XXV. The imitation of ancient forms accompanied the impulse toward realism. This reverence for older traditions gained the ascendancy in the sculpture of the Saite kings.

The Barkal statues have a feature which was inherited, apparently, from the technique of inlaying metal statues which flourished a little earlier. The granite was given a smooth polish except for surfaces which represented dress and ornament. Thus the cap, sandals, anklets, bracelets, and heavy necklaces, even the kilt, were left rough in order to hold better an application of gold leaf. The same surfaces were gilded on a small bronze figure of a king found at Gebel Barkal (No. 21.3096). This seems to be a more economical version of the inlaid metal details of the beautiful bronze statuettes of women in the Louvre and at Athens, or that of Osorkon I in the Brooklyn Museum. The technique, which was particularly developed in Dynasty XXII is well illustrated by the bronze aegis with a counterweight and head of Isis (No. 31.195). It is a type of sacred shoulder emblem known from sculptured figures and may in this case have been made for a statue.

102. Temple of Amon at Gebel Barkal

The sunk carvings of the gray granite altar of Atlanersa from Gebel Barkal follow in the tradition of the Dynasty XXV reliefs, such as those of the men leading Piankhy's horses in the same temple. The shape of the king's head resembles that in the Piankhy reliefs, or that of Psamtik and Nectanebo mentioned on p. 165, while the carefully delineated muscular structure of the bodies accords well with that realistic impulse to which reference has been made (Fig. 104). The representation is thoroughly Egyptian and is accompanied by correctly written hieroglyphic inscriptions, like those of the funerary stela of Aspelta (No. 21.347) from his pyramid chapel at Nuri. The king is shown on one face of the Atlanersa altar, standing on a platform supported by the plants of United Egypt which are being tied together by the gods Horus and Thoth. The upraised arms of the king are lifted to a conventional representation of the heavens. On the opposite side, Atlanersa stands in the same position flanked by two goddesses, who wear upon their heads the plants of Upper and Lower Egypt. Of course this symbolism of the king dominating the Two Lands was entirely misplaced in the time of Atlanersa who no longer controlled any part of Egypt. Nevertheless, it is continued on the other two faces of the altar by the Nile gods who again bind the heraldic plants, while above, the kneeling king is accompanied by the jackal-headed souls of Nekhen and the hawk-visaged spirits of Buto.

103. Detail of statue of Aspelta

104. Detail of Atlanersa altar (stand for bark of Amon)

The carvings on the enormous granite sarcophagus of King Aspelta (No. 23.-729) are not so fine in quality as those of the Atlanersa altar. They are cut in a more shallow sunk relief with less inner detail. The scheme of decoration is again thoroughly in the Egyptian tradition and not unlike the Dynasty XVIII coffin of Tuthmosis I (Fig. 68). The kneeling figures of goddesses appear upon the ends and the four genii of the dead in panels on the sides. To the latter have been added, however, flanking figures of Thoth, while the accompanying ritual texts are greatly increased, so that the whole surface of the huge receptacle is covered, inside and out, with closely spaced figures and hieroglyphs. The immense bulk of Aspelta's coffin is its most impressive feature.

The skill of the Napatan craftsmen is seen at its best in the wealth of funerary furniture, jewelry, and small objects found in the tombs of the Ethiopian kings. Perhaps the most beautiful, as well as one of the earliest of these pieces, is the

105. Gold and crystal ornament of a queen of Piankhy

106. Kushite ram's head ornaments: electrum sphinx on inlaid column, gold necklace pendant, crystal column with electrum head.

crystal ball surmounted by an exquisitely worked gold head of Isis wearing the horned disk (Fig. 105). This was found at El Kurru in the tomb of one of the queens of Piankhy. Equally magnificent is a little electrum statuette of a ram-headed sphinx set upon a column inlaid with colored stones, which came from the same tomb (Fig. 106). Similar in technique to these other precious ornaments is the electrum ram's head which caps a crystal column from another of the Kurru tombs (Fig. 106). With the objects of Piankhy's queen had been placed a blue-glazed bowl which, in its attractive shape and decoration, is closely allied to the contemporaneous work in Egypt. Four bulls are shown striding to the left around a central disk in the bottom of the bowl where the Hathor cow lies among papyrus reeds (Fig. 107). In the tomb of another queen of Piankhy, Neferuke-Kashta, was found a small silver statuette of Isis or Mut (No. 21.322), while the same queen is represented as being suckled by a goddess in a tiny silver relief (No. 24.928). From the tumulus of one of the ancestral chieftains who preceded Piankhy came a collar made of seven graduated rows of heavy gold ball beads, fitting close to the throat, and with a diamond-shaped pendant fused together

107. Faience bowl of a queen of Piankhy

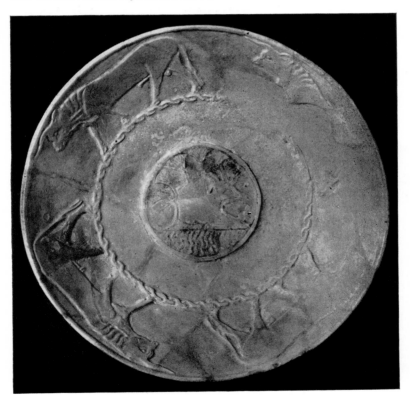

108. Bronze bed-leg of a queen of
     Shebitku

from smaller beads (No. 21.319). Another broad collar was made by joining two crescent shaped sheets of gold. It was worn by a queen of Shebitku and bears in front a winged figure of Isis in relief, while at the back is a scarab beetle (No. 21.-307). On another sheet of gold the name of Shabako is beaten out in raised hieroglyphs (No. 21.303).

Thus it is startlingly evident from many objects in this collection that the gold mines were still controlled by the Kushite kings, and the lavish use of the precious metal continues down through Meroitic times. Particularly magnificent in its soft color and graceful shape is the high-necked gold vase with a pointed base which came from the tomb of Aspelta, but of equally fine workmanship are the gold tweezers (No. 20.342) and the lid with its retaining chain of plaited gold from the same burial (No. 20.334). The gold ram's head of Analmaaye (Fig. 106) probably formed an element of such a heavy necklace as can be seen on our statues of Aspelta and Senkamanisken. The cylinder sheaths of electrum which belonged to Aspelta and to two later kings must have been valued highly, owing to the rarity of the silver which was mixed with the gold (Fig. 109). They are covered with minutely chased designs, the chief element of which is a standing figure of the goddess Isis with outstretched wings (Nos. 20.275, 21.339 to 341).

171

109. Electrum sheaths

110. Gilded silver mirror handle of Shabako

111. Gold breast pendant in the form of a winged Isis

Opposite: 112. Mirror with silver papyrus column handle

Their use is obscure. Of the time of King Shabako is the beautiful bronze mirror. The gilded silver handle (Fig. 110) is in the form of a palm column around the base of which project the figures of four gods, the irregularity in surface of their high relief giving a firm grasp for the hand. A mirror with a very similar silver handle, this time with a papyrus instead of a palm column, belonged to King Amani-nataki-lebte (No. 21.338; Fig. 112), in whose tomb was found the handsome gold pectoral in the form of a kneeling winged Isis (Fig. 111).

In Shabako's reign we find the first of the fascinating ivory carvings which also formed a notable part of the burial equipment of his successor Shebitku. A seated ivory lion, one of several which may have been playing pieces, was found in the king's own tomb (No. 24.1004), while in that of one of his queens were found the *djed*-patterns and paired papyrus flowers which evidently formed open-work elements of some piece of furniture (No. 24.1754). The delicately carved ivory reliefs of Shabako, which apparently decorated a box, remind us of such Saite ivories as a famous group in the Gulbenkian Collection. Whereas the Gulbenkian ivories clearly go back to Old Kingdom sources for their representations of offering bearers and animals, one group of the Shabako carvings has a graceful picturesque style the origin of which is to be sought in the New Kingdom. The same contrast between picturesque elements and the imitation of Old Kingdom forms occurs in the Neo-Memphite reliefs at the end of the Saite Period and again in the later tomb of Petosiris.

The Shabako ivories form fragments of panels in fine low relief, part of which are in Khartum. Offering bearers and men leading an ostrich are grouped between date palms in much the same way that palm trees separate the bound negro captives on the Tarquinia vase of Bocchoris, who was a contemporary of Shabako. On other pieces papyrus plants frame figures of men leading calves, or birds flying up as though from the marshes (No. 24.1018). Squatting figures of Nile gods, parts of palm columns, and a badly preserved seated king in a pavilion formed other elements in the decoration of the box (No. 24.1012). In a second group, the carving is not in relief but incised. Little figures brandishing weapons probably come from a hunting scene which is more clearly native Kushite, bearing even at its tiny scale a close relationship to the reliefs of Taharqa and such monuments as the altar of Atlanersa mentioned on p. 166. While some of the ivories of Shebitku are very like the first group of Shabako, with clumps of papyrus, men leading animals, and flying birds, others are on a larger scale. These represent figures of foreign prisoners in the same attitude and with the same careful details of costume as in the faience tiles of Ramesses III. Only Libyans and negroes are represented, and some of these have their bodies covered with a large crenelated cartouche containing the name of their tribe or locality, much as in the lists of foreign peoples on New Kingdom monuments.

The manufacture of objects in bronze had reached a perfection comparable to that of jewelry and ivory carving. From the tomb of Piankhy came a large offering table of fantastic design. A tall base shaped like an inverted horn tapers up to support a tray-like table. A palm column in the center holds a small bowl, while equally spaced on the rim of the table are four flower-shaped cups. These receptacles must have served for libations, the table perhaps containing the food and drink of the funerary meal. In the tomb of a queen of Shebitku was found a bronze leg of a funeral couch (Fig. 108). The base is in the form of a duck which rests upon a sloping-sided block ornamented with a design of papyrus flowers. The massive figure of the bird is a happy blending of realism and stylization. The surface of the body is covered with intricately incised feathering.

Of the other articles of funerary equipment, the most important is the complete series of shawabtis of the Kushite kings. The royal names included in the ritual texts on these figures have been of inestimable value in establishing the ownership of the pyramids at El Kurru and Nuri. By observing the changes in style and quality of workmanship it has been possible to establish the succession of these kings, many of whom were unknown before. Around the shawabtis could be arranged the groups of objects characteristic of each reign to give added support to this dating sequence. Like the Egyptian shawabtis from which these were derived, most of the Kushite figures were made of greenish faience, and as has been intimated above, they vary considerably in size and quality from reign to reign. The finest of all were those of Taharqa, which were carved from hard stone. Canopic jars bearing the name of the king or queen were recovered from many of the tombs, and several of these show fine carving in the heads of the four genii of the dead which appear upon their lids. Amongst the vessels and other objects carved from stone, a particularly attractive piece is the alabaster figure of a bound antelope which has horns of slate. This served as an ointment vase, and was found in one of the early graves at Meroë.

With a few of the objects of the later Kushite kings mentioned above we have progressed beyond the end of the Saite period, which came with the Persian invasion in 525 B.C., but many of the finest objects from Kush are contemporaneous, and all are closely bound up with the art of that time. It has usually been maintained that a renaissance in Egyptian art came as the result of a great upsurge of nationalistic feeling which accompanied the freeing of the country from the Assyrians. It is more probable that the main elements in the renewal of Egyptian culture are to be attributed to the new strength imparted to the country by the Kushite conquerors who had so recently been driven out by the Assyrians. It may be suggested that it was during the Kushite domination of Egypt that the real period of revival and experimentation occurred. The Saite craftsmen, after the brief interlude of Assyrian occupation, merely maintained, with a decreasing freshness of viewpoint and lessening force, what had been gained in Dynasty XXV.

The realism so evident in certain works of Dynasty XXV probably owed much to the rude vigor of the southern conquerors, who were closely enough related to the Egyptians to make the impulse seem sufficiently spontaneous. This has been implied in comparing the Cairo statues of Mentuemhat, the governor of Thebes,

Opposite: 114. Statue of King
Haker

113. Portrait of a priest

and Taharqa with our Kushite statues of a slightly later time. The superiority of technical skill was of course in the hands of the Egyptians and all these statues were probably made by Egyptian sculptors, but by men acting under new influences. Since Mentuemhat lived on into the reign of Psamtik I, some of his statues may have actually been made under that king, but the realistic strain in por · traiture soon decreased in Egypt itself. It is to be found again in the remarkable green head of a man (Fig. 113) which is one of a limited number of pieces the date of which has been much disputed. The head is later than the Saite Period, possibly falling into that time of Egyptian independence from the Persians which did not long precede the conquest of Alexander. The old Egyptian instinct to simplify the planes of the face is still at work here, but the bony structure of the skull, the wrinkles at the corners of the eyes, and the deeply etched line which runs from the base of the nostrils to the side of the mouth are handled with a remarkable perception of the aging features of an individual.

A simpler kind of realism which occasionally appears in work of the Late Period is to be seen in the black granite head (No. 37.377), or, on a somewhat minor scale, in the head of the standing male statue of dark stone (No. 07.494). The latter represents an outstanding characteristic of the period, the love of highly polished surfaces in very compact hard stones. This, perhaps more than any other feature, is what lends a cold quality to a great majority of examples of late sculpture. There is a certain lifelessness even in such faultlessly executed pieces as the smoothly carved green stone figure of Osiris from Giza (No. 29.1131) and the equally well-worked head in green stone (No. 04.1841). However there is magnificent modelling in the torso of King Haker, a rare monument of Dynasty

XXIX (Fig. 114). Routine conventionality combined with technical skill characterizes the numerous bronze figures of gods and animals of the late period, of which we possess fine examples in this collection.

Except in the simplicity of dress and traditional pose, there is little in the above statues to remind us of the use of Old Kingdom models upon which the Saite artists are supposed to have drawn for inspiration. That they deliberately copied early reliefs is clear from the craftswork scene of the tomb of Aba at Thebes, of the reign of Psamtik I, which was taken from that of an Old Kingdom noble of the same name at Deir el Gebrawi. It is probable also that Saite craftsmen drew the squares for copying over the reliefs of Zoser in a chamber under the Step Pyramid. Middle and New Kingdom models were also used but in the Theban tombs of Kushite and Saite officials the fine reliefs have an unexpected freshness and vitality, attractively exemplified by the little fragment of men boating in a swamp which may come from the tomb of Mentuemhat (Fig. 115). A more conventional work of the period, but with a remarkable portrait of the owner (Fig. 116), is the architrave with a worshipper before the family triads of Ptah and Osiris. The small reliefs, usually called Neo-Memphite, imitate Old Kingdom models in their processions of people bringing offerings to the dead man but have a very distinctive quality of their own. Nearly all the blocks have the same form, with long narrow friezes of figures topped by a rounded cornice. While some stones may have been the crowning decoration of a small rectangular structure containing a sarcophagus, others probably framed a doorway. They range in date from an undetermined time in the Saite Period down through Persian times to the first years of the Ptolemaic Period. Stylistic similarities relate them to such reliefs as those on our ivory carvings of Shabako, at the beginning of this range of time, and to the reliefs of the Hermopolis tomb of Petosiris at the end.

We have a charming small fragment of one of these reliefs which shows two women in a boat set against a picturesquely treated background of papyrus plants (Fig. 119). It is probably to be dated toward the end of the series, around 350 B.C., because of the Greek influence in the modelling of the bodies. The delicacy and charm of these reliefs make them the most appealing productions of late Egyptian art. The slightly exotic flavor of the later pieces owes something to the mingling of Egyptian and Greek forms, for once with happy result, but the whole series has antecedents also in the ivory carvings of the New Kingdom, in the *genre* scenes of the Theban tombs, and in the decorations of the bronze bowls of the late New Kingdom which were so often imitated by Phoenician craftsmen in later times. Something of the same spirit and style appears as late as the reign of Tiberius in some of the figures of women leading calves, and in the decorative arrangements of birds and flowers in the temple of Kom Ombo.

The contrast between the individuality of the Neo-Memphite reliefs and the conventional works of the time is as sharp as that between the green slate portrait (Fig. 113) and one of the smoothly polished routine heads. This can be seen

115. Men boating: relief from a Theban tomb. Dyn. XXV-XXVI

116. Portrait of owner: architrave from Memphite tomb. Dyn. XXVI

117. Granite relief of Nectanebo II

by comparing the fragment with the boating scene (Fig. 119) and a granite relief of Nectanebo II. This large granite block with the figures of a god and goddess in sunk relief was part of a construction erected by Nectanebo II at Bubastis (Fig. 117). It shows that Greek influence in the modelling, mentioned in the last paragraph, which has not been traced any earlier than Dynasty XXX. The familiar outlines of the figure remain, but the different parts of the body thus circumscribed are given an unusual roundness of modelling. The muscles of the abdomen are particularly prominent, while the peculiar pointed breast, which was to be characteristic of Ptolemaic figures, makes its appearance. In other examples, occasional foreshortenings are used somewhat inconsistently, particularly in the drawing of drapery. Although the traditional flat planes were much better suited to the linear character of the representation, it must be admitted that in this relief of Nectanebo II the modelling is so capably handled, particularly in the ram's-head of the god, that we can almost excuse the mixed character of the work.

180

118. Relief of Ptolemy I from Tarraneh

119. Neo-Memphite relief: girls boating

It is interesting to see this style develop. A fine example of early Ptolemaic work in limestone is the slab from Tarraneh (Fig. 118) with figures in low relief, but with the new development of the modelling of the bodies. A characteristic piece of temple decoration of one of the later Ptolemies is the gateway in sunk relief erected by Ptolemy VIII (Euergetes II) at Coptos (No. 24.1632). Here the precise workmanship of the Tarraneh piece, cold and conventional though it was, has given way to rather sloppy forms and carelessly made hieroglyphs

120. Attic Rhyton found at Meroë

121. Gold handle of a bowl from Daphnae

deeply sunk in the sandstone. Even these are more correctly drawn than the large inscriptions added by Nero on the lower part of the left-hand outer wall. The true Egyptian spirit has been lost in these late reliefs, which continue to recast the earlier forms in endless square yards of temple decoration in Ptolemaic and Roman times.

We have seen that, from the time of Nectanebo I on, there is a rather superficial mingling of Greek and Egyptian forms which, although it lent an attractive, exotic touch to the so-called Neo-Memphite reliefs, more frequently produced disastrous results. Ptolemaic art in general, however, follows two distinct main branches, either the pure Greek forms or a pedantic repetition of the old Egyptian types. Fine works in the Hellenistic tradition are represented in the Classical Collection of this Museum by the bronze head of the young Arsinoe II, the marble heads of Ptolemy IV and his wife Arsinoe III, and the faces on the beautiful Alexandrine coins. We are familiar with many Hellenistic objects which were imported into Egypt or found their way from Alexandria to the Meroitic court. But these were by no means the first imports from Greece. The Amazon rhyton of the Athenian potter Sotades (Fig. 120) goes back to the middle of the fifth century B.C. Sites like Daphnae and Naukratis have produced earlier evidence of the Greek traders and mercenaries settled there. To the time of the Greek mercenaries at Daphnae in the Saite Period, probably belongs the handsome gold handle of a dish with a decoration of palmettes, originally inlaid with colored stones or paste, Egyptian in character (Fig. 121). It was found by Petrie in the debris of the fort. At Memphis, where we remember that Amasis had settled some of the Greek troops from Daphnae, was found a limestone statue, now in Cairo, which was evidently made by a local sculptor in the last quarter of the sixth century. It imitates the type of archaic Greek maiden such as we know from the Athenian Acropolis. This, so far, is an isolated example of a very early mingling of Greek and Egyptian styles.

122. View of the Meroë pyramids

In the Sudan, the Egyptian style, although occasionally renewed by a fresh impetus from the north and influenced to a certain extent by the importation of classical objects, was gradually being submerged by African barbarism at Meroë (Fig. 122). It must be confessed that the blocks from the chapel of Pyramid N 51 at Meroë in the third century A.D. (Fig. 123) do not look very different from some work of the second century B.C.

The same heaviness appears in the smaller objects, but these show a mastery of craftsmanship far above that of the sculpture. The jewellers carried on the old traditions skillfully. The design is somewhat clumsier, the natural forms and human figures in the ornament are less well drawn than in the older Kushite pieces. Excellent examples of these rich ornaments are the earrings and bracelets. A new use was made of enamelled detail, as in the handsome bracelet (Fig. 125), or in some of the elaborately ornamented gold disks.

Of the objects imported from Alexandria into the Meroitic Kingdom there are several notable pieces. The earliest of these are two silver vessels from tombs in the southern cemetery at Meroë which belong to the first half of the third century B.C. One is a fluted bowl with high, flaring rim (No. 21.1041), while the other is a strainer with handles in the form of ducks' heads with gracefully curving necks (Fig. 124). Another group of Alexandrian vessels belongs to the first and second centuries A.D. The finest of these is a handsome silver cup with figures in high relief representing a scene of judgment (Fig. 126). An executioner and the judge seated on a raised dais can be easily recognized, but the meaning of the two children clutching at the knees of an excited woman, and the gesticulating man who accompanies them, is not so easily explained. It has been suggested that this forms a parallel to the Judgment of Solomon, perhaps one of the legends concerning the wise King Bocchoris which had a considerable vogue in Roman painting. Another plain silver cup has a different shape. It stands on a high base and is provided with slender curving handles (No. 24.876). A large bronze lamp has a spirited figure of a horse projecting from its handle (No. 24.-967), while a bronze vessel on a low base has, in the bottom of the bowl, a relief of Actaeon defending himself from the dogs (No. 24.979). Thoroughly classical in workmanship also is the head from a bronze statue with a wreath of vine leaves twined in the long locks of the man's hair (No. 24.957).

Also of Hellenistic-Roman workmanship and probably brought to Meroë from Alexandria are pieces of two rare glass vessels of the first century A.D. One, of clear dark blue glass, has a warrior with a shield and parts of two lions painted on it in gold (No. 21.11757). The other is a cup of clear green glass. On the bottom an Osiris head inside a flower garland is painted in several colors. Other figures were shown around the side in a Greek adaptation of Egyptian style (No. 21.11758).

Finally a word should be said about the polychrome painted pottery of Meroitic times. In addition to the wares with incised geometric decoration, a good deal of pottery with elaborately painted ornament has been found in the Sudan. The very light cups of buff-colored ware with crisply painted all-over patterns on the outside are the most characteristic of these vessels. Such a cup is that from the Meroitic Cemetery at Kerma with a pattern of *ankh*-signs resting on horn-shaped symbols (No. 13.4031) or others with hieroglyphic signs or stylized floral

123. Relief from a tomb chapel at Meroë

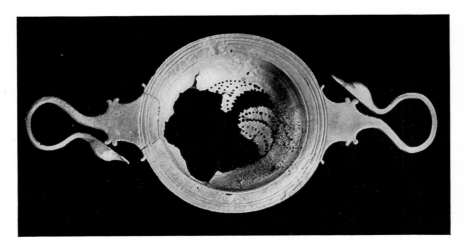

124. Silver strainer

motives in red, black, and brown against the light background. Two other vessels from the same cemetery bear more elaborate designs in brown, red, and dark purple, which are closely allied in style to the painted Coptic vessels of early Christian Egypt. One of these is a fragment from the upper part of a jar with an animated painting of a man being swallowed by a crocodile (No. 13.4035). The other is a narrow-necked pot, on the shoulder of which, above a garland of bunches of grapes, appears a row of crocodiles and a long-necked water bird (No. 13.4038).

One outstanding means of artistic expression in Roman Egypt was entirely Hellenistic in technique, although it was in line with the old pharaonic funerary practices. This was the painting of portrait heads, usually in the encaustic technique with hot wax, upon wooden panels which were inserted in the wrappings of the mummy. Two well-preserved mummies of the late second century A.D., one that of a young girl and the other of a bearded man (Nos. 11.2891, 2892), show how these heads looked, framed by their wrappings, when the body was ready to be escorted to the tomb. The painting in this case is of rather indifferent workmanship but three other panels show the masterly skill that was often expended upon these grave portraits. Nothing could be farther from the old Egyptian ideal than the full modelling, the play of light and shade, and the expressiveness of these three heads. They represent a change in fashions of dress and manner of painting from the lady with the Flavian curls of the late first century A.D. (No. 93.1451; Fig. 130) through the Hadrianic type of the bearded young man of the mid-second century A.D. (No. 02.825; Fig. 132) to the shaven dark-haired man of the second half of the second century A.D. (No. 93.1450). The plaster mummy masks of the first century A.D. are more conventionally treated, al-

186

125. Meroitic bracelet

126. Silver cup found at Meroë

127. Detail of mummy cloth of the lady Ta-sheret-wedja-hor

though the lady (No. 54.638; Fig. 128) wears her hair in the fashion of the Julio-Claudian family at the court in Rome. Quite different in character is the plaster mask of an old woman (No. 58.1196; Fig. 129) which is unusual for its qualities of portraiture. While it sharply portrays an individual of the second century A.D. the face anticipates that linear treatment which formed an Eastern element in late antiquity, rather than reflecting the Graeco-Roman plastic tradition. Most of these people are not portrayed as native Egyptians but belonged to the ruling class of foreigners and lived in the provincial towns of the Fayum and Upper Egypt in Roman times, undoubtedly intermarrying with the much larger body of the local populace. Sometimes, although the facial type is European, the name is Egyptian. This is so in the case of the woman Ta-sheret-wedja-hor who was married to the priest of Serapis and the wolf-god Wepwawet at Assiut. The inscription on her painted linen shroud (No. 54.993; Fig. 127) is dated to the 11th year of an unnamed emperor but the form of its demotic writing is thought to belong to a time shortly after the end of the Ptolemaic Period, early in the first century A.D. The bold expressive modelling of the face is like that of the figures in the Boscoreale frescoes in New York and the mummy portraits, also painted on linen, of the lady Aline and her two children in Berlin, who probably lived in the reign of Tiberius. Another painted cloth which covered the burial of a lady of the first century A.D. shows the same contrast between the beautifully executed

128. Plaster mask of young woman   129. Plaster mask of old woman

classical portrait and the badly conceived funerary iconography of the crudely drawn surrounding figures (No. 50.650; Fig. 133). These mummy cloths began to be used as early as Dynasty XXI when a profile figure of Osiris was outlined on the linen. Roman versions show the Osiris figure in front view, painted in several colors as in our No. 72.4724. Sometimes the owner is painted in the old Egyptian style in a tight-fitting sheath dress but with classical touches in the vine scrolls on her shoulder straps and the bier upon which she lies (No. 72.4723). Her headdress is probably made of twisted papyrus as in the case of an actual example of a papyrus funerary crown in our collection (No. 50.3788).

Gradually the linear style, and abstract Eastern approach to the representation of the human figure, which permeated Byzantine art, began to have its effect on the Hellenistic conception of portraiture. In the art of the Coptic Christian Egyptians this had its origin in an expression of popular feeling against the foreign ideas brought in by the ruling class. Carried almost to a ludicrous point, this last expression of the indigenous spirit can be seen in the crude bust of a mummy, painted and partly modelled in stuccoed linen (Fig. 131). The man is probably still a pagan, since the glass wine vessel and sprig of foliage do not necessarily denote Christian beliefs. This solemn male bust of the fourth century A.D. is as far in spirit from the sophisticated Fayum portraits as it is from its pharaonic predecessors.

130. *Left:* Encaustic portrait of young woman

131. *Right:* Late Roman mummy mask

132. *Below:* Encaustic portrait of
bearded man

133. Painted shroud with portrait of young woman

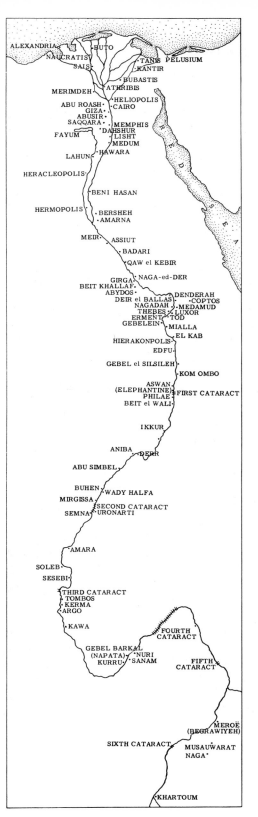

Map of Nile Valley

Egyptian Chronology

THE ARRANGEMENT of the Egyptian rulers into dynasties is based upon the History which the Egyptian priest Manetho prepared under Ptolemy II in the third century B.C. The Dynastic Lists have come down to us in the somewhat differing versions of the Christian writers Africanus and Eusebius of the third century A.D. while other passages of the History have been preserved in the work of Flavius Josephus of the first century A.D. (see W. G. Waddell, *Manetho*, The Loeb Classical Library, 1948). Several king lists, such as those which must have been employed by Manetho in preparing his History, have fortunately survived. The most important of these is the Turin Papyrus which was written in the reign of Ramesses II, but three other lists of the New Kingdom were inscribed upon monuments at Abydos, Saqqarah and Karnak. There is also a portion of the Annals of the early dynasties preserved on the Palermo Stone and its related fragments and prepared in Dynasty V. These can be supplementd by contemporaneous records referring to individual reigns, by biographical material from the monuments, the foreign correspondence of the Eighteenth Dynasty Amarna clay tablets, the Annals of Tuthmosis III and certain literary works which contain material useful for historical purposes.

The dating previous to Dynasty XII can be given only approximately. In the list of kings of the Turin Papyrus (G. Farina, *Il Papiro dei Re*, 1939, pp. 31-35), the length of the period from Menes to the end of Dynasty VIII is stated to be 955 years. The time from the beginning of Dynasty VI to the beginning of Dynasty IX is given as 187 years, while the length of Dynasty XI is 142 years. The uncertain factor, then, is the time from the end of Dynasty VIII to the beginning of Dynasty XI. In the following table, a length of about one hundred years has been allowed for this period (see W. S. Smith, " Evidence for the History of the Fourth Dynasty ", *Journal of Near Eastern Studies*, 11 (1952), pp. 113-122). It should be remembered that certain scholars would like to see this period shortened, while to others Dynasties I and II appear to occupy too long a time if the Turin figure of 955 years is accepted. The lengths of individual reigns are in part given from the figures preserved in the Turin Papyrus. These frequently can be supported by dates on contemporaneous monuments.

From the Middle Kingdom onwards, records have been preserved of a number of lunar dates and observations of the rising of the star Sothis (Sirius) in conjunction with the sun which has a cyclical recurrence at approximately every 1460 years. This material has been re-examined in recent years and has led to a number of slight changes in the dating of the Middle and New Kingdoms. Thus the beginning of Dynasty XII can be fixed more accurately at 1991 than the formerly accepted 2000 B.C., while the beginning of Dynasty XVIII should be pushed forward 10 years to 1570 from the 1580 B.C. which used to be employed. For Dynasty XII, I have followed the dates in Richard A. Parker's *The Calendars of Ancient Egypt* (1950). William F. Edgerton has proposed a number of alterations for Dynasty XVIII in an article " On the Chronology of the Early Eighteenth Dynasty (Amenhotep I to Thutmose III)", in *American Journal of Semitic Languages and Literatures*, 53 (1937), pp. 118-197. Other dates for the New Kingdom are taken from within the possible range of years for the beginning of each reign similarly calculated by Borchardt in *Die Mittel zur zeitlichen Festlegung von Punkten der ägyptischen Geschichte*, (1935).*

The beginning of Dynasty XXVI can be accurately fixed at 663 B.C., while the inscriptions relating to the burial of the Apis bulls give us fixed points for the reign of Taharqa in Dynasty XXV, Bocchoris of Dynasty XXIV and for the latter part of Dynasty XXII. Similar dates on the markings of the burials of the Theban priests and the re-burials of earlier kings provide a framework for Dynasty XXI but present problems which have not been entirely solved. It has seemed advisable for Dynasty XXI onward to follow the chronological table given by Drioton and Vandier in *L'Egypte* (1952), although the beginning of Dynasty XXII must fall after 950 if one accepts Albright's proposal of 922-915 for the reign of Rehoboam in whose fifth year Sheshonq I conquered Palestine (*Bulletin of the American Schools of Oriental Research*, 100 (1945), pp. 16 ff.). Drioton and Vandier have placed the fall of Jerusalem at about 930, while Breasted gave 926 B.C. Although it is generally assumed that Sheshonq attacked Palestine in his 20th year, it is only certain that this was before he carved a triumphal relief beside the gate at Karnak erected in his 21st year.

The comparative chronology of Egypt and Western Asia has been the subject of much discussion in recent years. Evidence is steadily accumulating from new excavations so that our information is in a state of constant growth requiring frequent revision of tentatively formed conclusions. This allows for considerable divergence of opinion but within ever narrowing limits as the gaps are gradually filled in. It is now generally assumed that the Djemdet Nasr Period in Mesopotamia corresponds roughly in time to that in Egypt called Protodynastic, leading into Dynasty I. The evidence of relations between the two countries remains of a somewhat tenuous nature and requires further clarification. There are many tangible signs of Egypt's contacts abroad in the Old and Middle Kingdoms but the underlying political situation is still obscure. At the end of the Middle Kingdom, when Egypt played no part in the affairs of northern Syria, a much clearer picture can be gained from the Mari letters. The chronological evidence, with its

---

* Richard A. Parker, in *Journal of Near Eastern Studies*, 16 (1957), pp. 39-43, now favors the lunar date of 1490 B.C. for the accession of Tuthmosis III and 1290 B.C. for that of Ramesses II. See also chronological table, W. C. Hayes, *The Scepter of Egypt*, II, 1959, pp. xiv, xv. Rowtan (*Journal of Near Eastern Studies*, 17 (1958), p. 100, note 24), on the other hand, recently suggests the date 1304 B.C. for Ramesses II.

bearing on the date of Hammurabi of Babylon, has been discussed in connection with the Khorsabad King List and the stratigraphy of a site in the Antioch Plain by Sidney Smith in *Alalakh and Chronology* (1940), and *American Journal of Archaeology*, 49 (1945), pp. 1-24. Albright has argued for a date considerably later than the 1792 B.C. assigned by Smith to Hammurabi and consequently a later date for Ashur Uballit, who corresponded with Akhenaten, as well as for Ramesses II (*Bulletin of the American Schools of Oriental Research*, 88 (1942), pp. 28-33; 118 (1950), p. 19; *American Journal of Archaeology*, 54 (1950), pp. 163, 170). The Egyptian evidence has also been re-examined in connection with the Khorsabad King List by M. B. Rowtan (*Iraq*, 8 (1946), pp. 94 ff.; *Journal of Egyptian Archaeology*, 34 (1948), pp. 57 ff.) who also proposes a later dating. Recently, Albrecht Goetze has protested against too low a dating of events between about 1650 and 1450 B.C., on the basis of Hittite evidence (*Bulletin of the American Schools of Oriental Research*, 122 (1951), pp. 18-25; *Journal of the American Oriental Society*, 72 (1952), pp. 67-72).

Therefore, it is doubtful, pending further investigation, that Egyptian dates should be altered to correspond to a lower chronology in Mesopotamia. This is especially so since E. Cavaignac and G. Goossens no longer accept the low date of 1728 for the beginning of the reign of Hammurabi (see Goossen's review of P. Van der Meer, *The Chronology of Ancient Western Asia and Egypt*, in *Bibliotheca Orientalis*, 13 (1956), pp. 191-192). M. B. Rowtan (*Journal of Near Eastern Studies*, 17 (1958), pp. 97 ff.) has also reconsidered the evidence and accepts Sidney Smith's dates of 1792-1750 B.C. for Hammurabi. It should be added that Landsberger and Goetze would like to see the date of Hammurabi pushed back even earlier (see *Journal of Cuneiform Studies*, 8 (1954), pp. 31-73, 106-133; 11 (1957), pp. 53-61, 63-73; *Bulletin of the American Schools of Oriental Research*, No. 127 (1952), p. 21; No. 146 (1957), p. 20).

PERIODS

PREHISTORIC:

> Before 4000: settlements in the Fayum, at Merimde-Beni-Salame and El Omari in Lower Egypt and at Tasa and Badari in Upper Egypt.

> 4000 B.C. to 3200 B.C.: the emergence from the stone age with the practical use of hardened copper.

>> *Amratian:* also called Early Predynastic or Naqadah I: Petrie's Sequence Dates (SD 30-40)

>> *Gerzean:* also called Naqadah II
>> Early Gerzean (SD 40-50): corresponds to Middle Predynastic.
>> Late Gerzean (SD 50-79): includes the ill-defined corpus of objects formerly termed Semainean or Late Predynastic and the transitional period leading up to Dynasty I sometimes called Protodynastic (including King Scorpion).

For a new survey of Prehistoric Egypt, see Werner Kaiser, ' Stand und Probleme der ägyptischen Vorgeschichtsforschung ', *Zeitschrift für Aegyptische Sprache und Altertumskunde*, 81 (1956), pp. 87-109. See also Helene J. Kantor, ' The Final Phase of Predynastic Culture, Gerzean or Semainean (?)', *Journal of Near Eastern Studies*, 3 (1944), 110-136, and in Robert W. Ehrich, *Relative Chronologies in Old World Archaeology*, Chicago, 1954, p. 1 ff. For sites in the eastern Delta, see Henry G. Fischer, 'A Fragment of Late Predynastic Relief from the Eastern Delta ', *Artibus Asiae*, 21 (1958), pp. 64-88.

ARCHAIC PERIOD: 3200 to 2680 B.C.

Dynasty I: 3200–2980 B.C.
Narmer ⎫
Aha ⎬ Menes
Zer (Ity): 19 + years
Zet
Wedymu (Khasety)
Az-ib (Mer-pa-ba): 20 + years
Semerkhet (Shemsu ?): 9 years
Qay-a (Sen-mu)

Dynasty II: 2980–2780 B.C.
Ra-neb
Hetep-sekhemuwy
Netery-mu (Ny-neter): 22 + years
Peribsen (Sekhem-ib Per-en-maat)
Sened
Khasekhem
Khasekhemuwy: 17 years

Dynasty III: 2780–2680 B.C.
Sa-nekht
Neterkhet (Zoser)
Sekhem-khet
Kha-ba (Tety)
Neb-ka (Neb-ka-ra)
Huni (Hu): 24 years

OLD KINGDOM: 2680 to 2258 B.C.

Dynasty IV: 2680–2565 B.C.
Sneferu: 24 years
Cheops (Khufu): 23 years
Radedef: 8 years
Chephren (Khafra): 25 (?) years
Bikheris: 1 (?) year
Mycerinus (Menkaura): 28 (?) years
Shepseskaf: 4 years
Thampthis: 2 years

Dynasty V: 2565–2420 B.C.
    Weserkaf: 7 years
    Sahura: 14 years
    Neferirkara: 10 years
    Shepseskara (Isy): 7 years
    Neferefra: ? years
    Ne-user-ra: 30 (?) years
    Men-kau-hor: 8 years
    Isesy (Zedkara): 39 (?) years
    Unas: 30 years

Dynasty VI: 2420–2258 B.C.
    Tety: 12 years
    Weserkara: 1 (?) year
    Pepy I: 49 years: Mernera probably co-regent in Pepy's 40th year.
    Mernera: 14 (?) years; 5 years of reign alone.
    Pepy II: 94 (?) years
    Mernera II: 1 year

FIRST INTERMEDIATE PERIOD: 2258 to 2040 B.C.

Dynasty VII: Interregnum

Dynasty VIII: (Memphite) 2258–2232

Dynasty IX: (Heracleopolitan) 2232–2140 B.C.
    Khety I (Mer-ib-ra)
    13 kings of Turin Papyrus (including Khety II)

Dynasty X: (Heracleopolitan) 2140–2040 B.C.
    Neferkara
    Khety III (Wah-ka-ra)
    Merikara
    Khety IV (Neb-kau-ra)

        Contemporaneous with Dynasty X:
            Dynasty XI in South: 2134–2040
                Mentuhotep I (Tepy-aa) ⎱
                Intef I (Seher-tawy) ⎰ 2134–2118
                Intef II (Wah-ankh): 2118–2068
                Intef III (Nekht-neb-tep-nefer): 2068–2061
                Mentuhotep II (Neb-hepet-ra): 2061–2040
                    (who bore Horus names Se-ankh-ib-tawy, Neter-hedjet,
                    Sema-tawy*)

Fall of Heracleopolis to Mentuhotep II: 2040

---

*For the kings of Dynasty XI: see A. H. Gardiner, *Mitteilungen des Deutschen Archaologisches Institut, Kairo,* 14 (1956), pp. 42–51; Labib Habachi, *Annales du Service des Antiquités de l'Egypte,* 55 (1958), pp. 178–185.

MIDDLE KINGDOM: 2040 to 1786 B.C.

Dynasty XI: United Egypt: 2040–1991
    Mentuhotep II: 2040–2010
    Mentuhotep III (Se-ankh-kara): 2010–1998
    Civil wars plus short reign of
        Mentuhotep IV (Neb-tawy-ra): 1998–1991

Dynasty XII: 1991–1786 B.C.
    Amenemhat I (Sehetep-ib-ra): 1991–1962
    Sesostris I (Kheper-ka-ra): 1971–1928
    Amenemhat II (Neb-kau-ra): 1929–1895
    Sesostris II (Kha-kheper-ra): 1897–1878
    Sesostris III (Kha-kau-ra): 1878–1842
    Amenemhat III (Ny-maat-ra): 1842–1797
    Amenemhat IV (Maat-kheru-ra): 1798–1789
    Queen Sebek-neferura: 1789–1786

SECOND INTERMEDIATE PERIOD: 1786 to 1570 B.C.

Dynasties XIII–XIV: 1786–1680
    Period of political disintegration: circa 30 kings

Dynasties XV–XVI (Hyksos): 1720–1570 B.C.
(Local rulers at Thebes forming Dynasty XVI)
    Khian (Se-weser-en-ra)
    Apepi (Aa-weser-ra)
    Apepi (Neb-khepesh-ra)
    Aa-seh-ra
    Apepi (Aa-kenen-ra)

Dynasty XVII: 1600-1570 B.C.
    Taa-aa
    Taa-ken (Sekenenra)
    Kamose (Waz-kheper-ra)

NEW KINGDOM: 1570 to 1085 B.C.

Dynasty XVIII: 1570–1349
    Ahmose I: 1570–1545
    Amenhotep I: 1545–1525
    Tuthmosis I: 1525–1508
    Tuthmosis II: 1508–1504
    Hatshepsut: 1504–1483
    Tuthmosis III: 1504–1450
    Amenhotep II: 1450–1423
    Tuthmosis IV: 1423–1410
    Amenhotep III: 1410–1372
    Akhenaten: 1372–1355
    Semenkhkara ⎫
    Tut-ankh-amon ⎬ 1355–1342
    Ay ⎭

Dynasty XIX: 1342–1197
   Horemheb: 1342–1314
   Ramesses I: 1314–1313
   Sety I: 1313–1301
   Ramesses II: 1301–1234
   Merenptah: 1234–1222
   Amen-meses: 1222
   Siptah (Merenptah): 1222–1216
   Sety II: 1216–1210
   Siptah (Ramesses) ⎫
   Irsu (?)   ⎬ 1210–1197

Dynasty XX: 1197–1085
   Sety-nekht: 1197–1195
   Ramesses III: 1195–1164
   Ramesses IV–XI: 1164–1085

PERIOD OF DECLINE: 1085 to 663 B.C.

Dynasty XXI: (Tanite Dynasty; priest kings in Thebes) 1085–950 B.C.
   Smendes   ⎧
   Herihor (Thebes) ⎨ 1085–1054

   Psusennes I (Pasebkhanu) ⎫
   Paynozem (Thebes)   ⎬ 1054–1009
   Amen-em-ipet: 1009–1000
   Sa-amon: 1000–984
   Psusennes II (Pasebkhanu): 984–950

Dynasty XXII: (Bubastite) 950–730 B.C.: Libyan kings
   Sheshonq I: 950–929
   Osorkon I: 929–893
   Takelot I: 893–870
   Osorkon II: 870–847
   Sheshonq II: 847
   Takelot II: 847–823
   Sheshonq III: 823–772
   Pami: 772–767
   Sheshonq V: 767–730

      Partly contemporaneous with Dynasty XXII:
         Dynasty XXIII: 817 (?)–730 B.C.
            Dates only approximate for following kings.
            Pedibast: 817–763
            Sheshonq IV: 763–757
            Osorkon III: 757–748
            Takelot III   ⎫
            Rud-amon   ⎬ 748–730
            Osorkon IV ⎭

Dynasty XXIV: 730–715 B.C.
   Tef-nekht: 730–720
   Bocchoris (Bakenrenef): 720–715

Partly contemporaneous with Dynasties XXIII–XXIV:
Dynasty XXV: (Kushite: Ethiopian) 751–656 B.C.
Kashta
Piankhy: 751–716; Conquest of Egypt: Circa 730
Shabako: 716–701
Shebitku: 701–690
Taharqa: 690–664
Tanwetamani: 664–653

Assyrians in Egypt: 671 sack of Memphis under Esarhaddon; 663 sack of Thebes by Ashurbanipal; 658–651 Psamtik I gains control of country.

SAITE PERIOD: 663 to 525 B.C.

Dynasty XXVI: 663–525 B.C.
Psamtik I (Wah-ib-ra): 663–609
Necho (Nekau, Wehem-ib-ra): 609–594
Psamtik II (Nefer-ib-ra): 594–588
Apries (Haa-ib-ra): 588–568
Amasis (Ahmes-sa-neith, Khnum-ib-ra): 568–525
Psamtik III (Ankh-ka-en-ra): 525

FOREIGN DOMINATION

PERSIAN PERIOD: 525 to 332 B.C.

Dynasty XXVII: 525–404 B.C. FIRST PERSIAN DOMINATION:

Cambyses: 525–522
Darius I: 522–485
Xerxes: 485–464
Artaxerxes I: 464–424
Darius II: 424–404

Dynasty XXVIII: 404–398 B.C.
Amyrtaios: 404–398

Dynasty XXIX: 398–378 B.C.
Nepheritis I (Naifaaurud): 398–392
Akhoris (Haker): 392–380
Psammouthis (Psamut): 380–379
Nepheritis II (Naifaaurud): 379–378

Dynasty XXX: 378–341 B.C.
Nectanebo I: (Nekht-nebef) 378–360
Teos: 361–359
Nectanebo II (Nekht-hor-heb): 359–341

Dynasty XXXI: 341–332 B.C. SECOND PERSIAN DOMINATION:
Artaxerxes III (Ochos): 341–338
Arses: 338–335
Darius III (Codoman): 335–330

PTOLEMAIC PERIOD: 332–30 B.C.

    Alexander the Great: 332–323
    Ptolemy I (Soter): 323–283
    Ptolemy II (Philadelphus): 283–246
    Ptolemy III (Euergetes I): 246–221
    Ptolemy IV (Philopator): 221–205
    Ptolemy V (Epiphanes): 205–180
    Ptolemy VI (Philometor): 180–145 (Joint rule with Euergetes II: 170–163)
    Ptolemy VII (Neos Philopator): 145 (Eupator also in 145)
    Ptolemy VIII (Euergetes II): 145–116
    Ptolemy IX (Soter II): 116–108, 88–80
    Ptolemy X (Alexander): 108–88
    Ptolemy XI (Alexander): 80
    Ptolemy XII (Auletes): 80–51
    Ptolemy XIII: 51–48
      Cleopatra VII
    Ptolemy XIV: 47–44
      Cleopatra VII
    Cleopatra VII: 43 (?)–30
      Ptolemy XV (Caesarion)

ROMAN PERIOD: 30 B.C. to A.D. 324 (Accession of Constantine)

BYZANTINE OR COPTIC PERIOD: A.D. 324–640.

CHRONOLOGY OF KUSH (ETHIOPIA)

1. Period of the Egyptian trading caravans: 2400 to 2260 B.C.

2. Period of expanding economic and political control beginning in Dynasty XII: Egyptian administrative colony at Kerma: 2000 to 1680 B.C.

3. Absorption of Kush by the civil administration of Egypt: the twenty-four Egyptian viceroys of Kush: the Egyptianization of Kush 1540 to 1100 B.C.

4. Period of the ancestors of the royal family of Kush: seizure of the trade routes and the city of Napata: 900 to 750 B.C.

5. THE NAPATAN KINGDOM OF KUSH: 751 to 542 B.C.

    a. The first two kings, Kashta and Piankhy, conquer Egypt.

    b. Shabako (716–701 B.C.), Shebitku (701–690 B.C.), Taharqa (690–664 B.C.) and Tanwetamani (664–653 B.C.) rule Egypt and Ethiopia as Egyptian Dynasty XXV: First Napatan Dynasty; expelled from Egypt by the Assyrians.

    c. Second Napatan Dynasty: ruled Kush only (653–542 B.C.) Descendants of Taharqa: Atlanersa (653–643 B.C.), Senkamanisken (643–623 B.C.), Anlamani (623–593 B.C.), Aspelta (593–568 B.C.), and two other kings. Seat of government and principal residence at Napata. Secondary residence at Meroë.

201

6. THE MEROITIC KINGDOM OF KUSH: 542 B.C. to A.D. 339.

    a. First Phase: King Analmaaye to King Nastasen (542–337 B.C.). Seat of government and royal residence at Meroë. Burial of kings at Napata.

    b. Second Phase: Seven kings (337–248 B.C.). Concentration of power at Meroë. Kings buried at Meroë. Napata retains importance only for its sanctuary of Amon.

    c. Third Phase: Eighteen kings and ruling queens (Candaces) (248 B.C.–A.D. 41). Flowering of Meroitic culture. Great building period.

    d. Fourth Phase: Twenty-two or more kings (A.D. 41–339). Period of slow decline and degeneration of Meroitic culture, terminating in the destruction of Meroë.

Index